Cambridge Elements

Elements in Metaphysics
edited by
Tuomas E. Tahko
University of Bristol

LAWS OF NATURE

Tyler Hildebrand
Dalhousie University

Shaftesbury Road, Cambridge CB2 8EA, United Kingdom

One Liberty Plaza, 20th Floor, New York, NY 10006, USA

477 Williamstown Road, Port Melbourne, VIC 3207, Australia

314–321, 3rd Floor, Plot 3, Splendor Forum, Jasola District Centre,
New Delhi – 110025, India

103 Penang Road, #05–06/07, Visioncrest Commercial, Singapore 238467

Cambridge University Press is part of Cambridge University Press & Assessment,
a department of the University of Cambridge.

We share the University's mission to contribute to society through the pursuit of
education, learning and research at the highest international levels of excellence.

www.cambridge.org
Information on this title: www.cambridge.org/9781009111126
DOI: 10.1017/9781009109949

First published 2023

A catalogue record for this publication is available from the British Library.

ISBN 978-1-009-11112-6 Paperback
ISSN 2633-9862 (online)
ISSN 2633-9854 (print)

Laws of Nature
Elements in Metaphysics

DOI: 10.1017/9781009109949
First published online: February 2023

Tyler Hildebrand
Dalhousie University

Author for correspondence: Tyler Hildebrand, ty214256@dal.ca

Abstract: This Element provides an opinionated introduction to the metaphysics of laws of nature. The first section distinguishes between scientific and philosophical questions about laws and describes some criteria for a philosophical account of laws. Subsequent sections explore the leading philosophical theories in detail, reviewing the most influential arguments in the literature. The final few sections assess the state of the field and suggest avenues for future research.

Keywords: laws of nature, Humeanism, Non-Humeanism/Anti-Humeanism, metaphysics, philosophy of science

ISBNs: 9781009111126 (PB), 9781009109949 (OC)
ISSNs: 2633-9862 (online), 2633-9854 (print)

Contents

1 Introduction

1.1 Scientific vs. Metaphysical Questions about Laws

Nature is full of regularities. Some are obvious: that bread nourishes, that heavy objects are attracted to the earth, and so on. Others, such as the patterns described by Schrödinger's equation or Einstein's field equations, are much harder to discover but more resilient. Indeed, we take them to be necessary: it's no accident that oppositely charged particles attract; under normal conditions, they *must* attract. Such regularities are associated with *laws of nature*.

Laws of nature are a subject of interest for both science and philosophy. However, scientists and philosophers focus on different aspects of laws. Scientists are primarily interested in *which* laws of nature there are. For example, physicists ask questions such as: What are the values of various physical constants? Is gravity Newtonian or relativistic? Should we accept classical or quantum mechanics? To clarify, let's take a closer look at the third question.

Classical Mechanics: The behavior of fundamental things is described by Newton's laws of motion.

Quantum Mechanics: The behavior of fundamental things is described by the laws of quantum mechanics, such as the Schrödinger equation.

These theories agree that laws describe the motions of objects. However, their laws differ, so they posit different regularities at the more fundamental levels of nature.

In contrast, philosophers are interested in metaphysical questions about the *nature* of laws. They ask questions such as: What kind of thing is a law? What makes some regularities lawlike and others accidental? Why does nature contain regularities in the first place?[1]

A thought experiment will help to motivate some different answers to these metaphysical questions.

Virtual Physicists: The departments of Physics and Computer Science have collaborated to produce a video game, *Virtual Physicists*. The objective is to explore a simulated environment, make observations, collaborate with other players, and together formulate a scientific theory that explains and predicts events in the virtual world. The game ends when the players discover the true final theory: the set of lawlike generalizations and boundary conditions in the program running the simulation.

---

[1] We'll see later (especially in Section 9) that philosophers are interested in other sorts of questions about laws, too.

Your task in the game is to answer *scientific* questions about laws. (It's not called "Virtual Philosophers"!) But suppose we ask why the virtual world contains regularities as opposed to irregularities. The answer is obvious: The regularities – namely, patterns on your screen – are *not* simply a rock-bottom stopping point for explanation, nor do they occur purely by chance; rather, they are *imposed* on the virtual environment by the program and ultimately by the programmers/developers.

The nature of laws in our world might be analogous or it might not be. Everyone agrees that laws and regularities are intimately related. However, the central metaphysical dispute about laws concerns the nature of this relationship. Compare:

Humeanism: The world is like a grand mosaic whose tiles could have been arranged any which way. Nothing is ultimately responsible for its regularities. They are just a basic, fundamental feature of our world. Statements of laws, then, are merely descriptions of the most significant regularities that happen to occur. Thus, our world is *not* analogous to the worlds in *Virtual Physicists.*[2]

Non-Humeanism: The world is like a grand mosaic, but it's *not* the case that its tiles could have been arranged any which way. Something imposes structure on it, analogously to the way in which the computer program *Virtual Physicists* imposes structure on its virtual environments. For example, some Non-Humeans posit a god as the enforcer of natural laws, some treat laws as primitives, and there are other options besides. But whatever the details, all Non-Humeans accept some sort of basic, fundamental necessity: something that governs, produces, or somehow constrains patterns of events in nature.[3]

This philosophical dispute concerns the nature of laws (or natural necessities) and the order of metaphysical explanation: Humeans hold that regularities are prior to laws (or any other sort of natural necessity), whereas Non-Humeans hold that laws (or some natural necessities) are prior to regularities. Generally speaking, Humeans and Non-Humeans can agree about *which* sentences are statements of laws – a matter left to scientists – while disagreeing about what makes them lawlike.

Of course, there are also disputes internal to Humeanism and Non-Humeanism. For example, I said in this section that Humeanism takes the most

---

[2] This view is so called because David Hume (1748/2000) famously argued that the concept of natural necessity had to be analyzed in terms of observed patterns. However, it's controversial whether Hume endorsed Humeanism as I've defined it (Strawson, 2015).

[3] The terms 'Non-Humean' and 'Anti-Humean' are used interchangeably in the literature. I prefer 'Non-Humean'. As I've said elsewhere (Hildebrand, 2020b), although I'm not a Humean, I'm not *anti*-Humean!

significant regularities to be laws, but the notion of significance is open to interpretation. This leads to different versions of Humeanism. Similarly, there are many versions of Non-Humeanism, differing with respect to the primitive necessities they posit. Some appeal to God, some treat laws themselves as primitive, some invoke special sorts of properties, and so on. We'll explore narrower versions of both theories in later sections.

1.2 Philosophical Method

As noted, Humeanism and Non-Humeanism are typically formulated in an effort to accommodate our best scientific theories of laws. That seems to suggest that our metaphysical theories will be empirically equivalent. How, then, are we to choose one?

In comparison, it might seem easy to settle scientific disputes about laws. Precisely because scientific disputes about laws are disputes about *which* laws (and thus *which* regularities) there are, we can settle them by careful observation. However, even the question "How do we choose a scientific theory?" is difficult to answer. Consider the apparent position of stars during the famous Eddington experiment in 1919. Newtonian theories of gravity (of the day) and Einstein's theory of gravity made different predictions about where stars would appear during a solar eclipse. Eddington's team looked at the stars and found the predictions of Einstein's theory to be more accurate. Did everyone immediately accept Einstein's theory over Newton's? No. Newtonian theories could be modified to make predictions matching the observations of the experiment. Thus, Newtonian theories could be made empirically equivalent to Einstein's theory, at least for known observations of the day. How, then, can scientists justify a choice among empirically equivalent theories?

The answer, in short, is that scientists can and do appeal to *nonempirical theoretical virtues*. For example, Einstein's theory seems simpler and more elegant than its empirically equivalent Newtonian competitors. Generally speaking, *nonempirical criteria for theory choice* are required to solve problems of empirical underdetermination.

Analogously, philosophers appeal to similar criteria for theory choice when doing metaphysics.[4] I'll provide a brief sketch of some important criteria, but it includes a strong disclaimer. In this section, I won't try to justify them or say how they fit together to form a big-picture method for metaphysics. I'll say a bit more about this in Sections 8 and 9, after we've seen how the criteria are employed in philosophical practice.

---

[4] For defenses of metaphysics that proceed along these sorts of lines, see Paul (2012), Sider (2011, 11–15), and Tahko (2015).

For starters, a theory of laws should be intelligible; it shouldn't involve primitive concepts that we cannot understand. For example, Non-Humeans need to explain how we come to possess the concept of primitive necessity that features in their theories.

Theories should be simple and/or parsimonious. They shouldn't posit too many (kinds of) entities when fewer (kinds of) entities will do.

Theories of laws should cohere with scientific practice concerning laws and align with the ordinary concept of laws. Every philosophical analysis must start somewhere. If our account of laws is to be an account of *laws* – the things scientists talk about when they use the term – the account should classify the things we call "laws" as laws, and it should accommodate at least some of our normal intuitions about the work laws are supposed to do. For example, a metaphysical account of laws should make sense of the fact that scientists appeal to laws to explain observations and make predictions.

Relatedly, it would be nice if a theory of laws could explain *why* there are regularities in nature. But providing such explanations can be difficult, in part because some explanations merely push the problem back a level. If we posit a new entity to explain a regularity, we can ask why that new entity is the way that it is. We don't want to posit "turtles all the way down."

Finally, an account of lawhood should fit within our broader metaphysics. A metaphysical naturalist – one who thinks that nothing exists beyond the world of spacetime – would find it costly to endorse a theory of laws that posits a god. But if your metaphysics of laws fits seamlessly within your broader metaphysical commitments, that would be a mark in its favor.

In sum, there are many criteria relevant to the selection of a philosophical theory of laws. We'll examine them more carefully in due course, but this overview should provide a sufficient foundation to get started.

1.3 Why Care?

To conclude this section, I'll briefly mention some ways in which philosophical reflection on the nature of laws might be valuable.

First, science is one of the best things humans have created. That makes it worthy of philosophical reflection, if only for our own curiosity and enjoyment. More importantly, because science is valuable to us, it's worth trying to understand how scientific theories are to be interpreted; it's worth asking why science has the virtues it has and why it's possible for beings like us. Answers to such questions require us to say at least something about the nature of laws.

Second, the metaphysics of laws intersects with other philosophical issues. Generally speaking, an account of the nature of the world is relevant to accounts of how we ought to form our beliefs and live our lives. Only one connection of this sort is discussed in this Element (Sections 3.4, 8, and 9), but it's important: Laws are essential for *induction*, the form of inference – crucial to both science and ordinary life – in which we make predictions about the unobserved on the basis of the observed.

Third, studying philosophy can teach us humility. A better understanding of what laws might be helps us to understand our limitations and the strengths and weaknesses of scientific methods. Occasionally, a prominent scientist will make disparaging remarks about philosophy (I won't name names). I think this reflects a failure to understand the nature of scientific or philosophical projects, as well as the relations between them. Historically, science and philosophy have been viewed as complementary by leading scientists (e.g., Newton and Einstein).

Unfortunately, I don't have much space to discuss questions of value in this Element. However, my hope is that exposure to philosophical questions themselves will help readers to see the value for themselves. So, let's dive in. We'll begin with a careful examination of Humeanism.

2 Humeanism

At the fundamental level, Humeanism doesn't posit any primitive necessity or other modally robust primitives; it just posits non-modal events in spacetime – i.e., *the Humean mosaic*. That's all. Its ontology (the entities that exist according to the theory) is economical, and its conceptual primitives (the primitive predicates required to express the theory) are easily grasped. In contrast, Non-Humeans posit primitive necessities in addition to events in spacetime. But why worry about exotic metaphysical necessities if we don't have to? In this section, we'll examine some different versions of Humeanism.

To begin, here was our initial statement of Humeanism:

Humeanism: The world is like a grand mosaic whose tiles could have been arranged any which way. Nothing is ultimately responsible for its regularities. They are just a basic, fundamental feature of our world. Statements of laws, then, are merely descriptions of the most significant regularities that happen to occur…

There are two distinct claims here: first, that nature consists of a "Humean mosaic"; second, that laws are, or reduce to, regularities in the Humean mosaic. We'll spend the bulk of our efforts examining the second claim, but I'll say a little more about the Humean mosaic before we begin.

2.1 The Humean Mosaic

I have provided a *negative* characterization of the Humean mosaic, in terms of its lack of primitive necessities. However, many Humeans would prefer a *positive* characterization – one that tells us what the mosaic is like without invoking any modal language at all. As we'll see in Section 5, some Humeans maintain that we don't understand the modal language invoked in Non-Humean theories. It would be a problem if their own theory required the same language.

Here is an example of a positive characterization due to David Lewis:

> We have geometry: a system of external relations of spatiotemporal distance between points. … And at those points we have local qualities: perfectly natural intrinsic properties which need nothing bigger than a point at which to be instantiated. For short: we have an arrangement of qualities. And that is all. (Lewis, 1986b, ix)

Lewis doesn't invoke any modal language, but he does tell us more about the fundamental properties instantiated by points in the mosaic. They are *perfectly natural*, *intrinsic*, *point-sized*, and so on. Don't worry if you're not familiar with these concepts. What matters for present purposes is just that these concepts aren't supposed to have primitive modal character. The upshot is that it does seem possible to provide a positive characterization of the Humean mosaic.

However, the details are controversial. For example, Lewis's characterization seems unable to accommodate entangled states of quantum mechanics, since such states seem to involve connections between distinct points of the Humean mosaic (Maudlin, 2007). If that's right, Lewis's account of the Humean mosaic is incompatible with one of our best scientific theories. There are various proposals for characterizing the Humean mosaic that seek to avoid this problem, but this is largely an internal dispute among Humeans and unfortunately there isn't space to consider them here.[5]

What matters for our purposes is that Humeans are united in their rejection of primitive modality. Thus, we'll stick with a negative characterization of the Humean mosaic. This gives Humeans freedom to adjust their positive characterization of the mosaic to match our best scientific theories, and it will suit us just fine in our attempt to understand the major differences between Humeanism and Non-Humeanism. Namely, it suffices to make sense of one of the primary motivations for seeking a Humean theory of laws: Its ontology is economical and its conceptual resources (whatever they turn out to be) will be easier to understand insofar as they do not invoke primitive modality. Let's shift our attention to the claim that laws are analyzed in terms of regularities.

---

[5] See, for example, Loewer (1996), Earman and Roberts (2005a), and Bhogal and Perry (2017).

2.2 The Naïve Regularity Theory

Suppose the world is a Humean mosaic. According to Humeanism, laws are, or reduce to, regularities. But not just any regularities will do. They have to be "significant." What does that mean, and why should we restrict lawhood to significant regularities in the first place?

Well, here are some statements that do *not* seem lawlike:

(1) Most elementary particles have mass.
(2) All electrons have positive charge.
(3) The result of adding 2 and 2 is always 4.
(4) On January 1, 2022, all the books on my desk were written by David Armstrong.

Each statement describes a regularity. Why, then, aren't they statements of laws? Statement (1) isn't universal, but we typically think of (fundamental) laws as holding at all times and places. Statement (2) is false, which seems to disqualify it. Statement (3) is necessarily true. However, mathematical necessity seems stronger than natural necessity. We can't imagine worlds in which $2 + 2 \neq 4$, but we *can* imagine worlds with different laws. Finally, statement (4) is tied to specific people, places, and times. The laws of respectable scientific theories aren't – at least not at more fundamental levels of science.

Each statement suggests a condition on lawhood, giving rise to the following Humean theory:

The Naïve Regularity Theory: *L* is a *statement of a law of nature* if and only if *L* is (i) universally quantified, (ii) true, (iii) contingent, and (iv) contains only nonlocal empirical predicates apart from logical connectives and quantifiers.[6]

Notice that we have replaced the vague term 'significant' with a more precise set of conditions.

The Naïve Regularity Theory has some attractive features. Because its language is precise and it avoids reference to mysterious primitives, it fares well with respect to the virtues of conceptual clarity and ontological economy. Also, its classification of laws seems accurate. According to this theory, none of (1)–(4) are statements of laws, whereas paradigm statements of law such as the Schrödinger equation *are*.

---

[6] This statement is borrowed with slight modifications from Armstrong (1983, 12), who borrowed it from Molnar (1969, 79).

2.3 Extensional Problems for the Naïve Regularity Theory

Unfortunately, the Naïve Regularity Theory has a serious problem: It is *extensionally inadequate*, which is to say that it fails to correctly classify statements of laws. In other words, the expressions on either side of the 'if and only if' pick out different classes. We'll illustrate with two counterexamples.

The following two statements suggest that conditions (i)–(iv) are *insufficient* for lawhood.

(1) All solid spheres of Uranium-235 have radius < 1 km.
(2) All solid spheres of gold have radius < 1 km.

Both statements meet all four of the Naïve Regularity Theory's conditions on lawhood: they are universally quantified, true, contingent, and avoid local predicates. Thus, the theory classifies both as statements of laws. But, intuitively, only (1) is a statement of law. There *couldn't* be a large sphere of Uranium-235, because it would exceed the critical mass. In contrast, (2) seems *accidental*. There are no large spheres of gold, but there could have been. Nothing about the nature of gold would prevent the formation of a large gold sphere. Thus, the theory implies that (2) is a statement of law when in fact it isn't.

This is an example of *the problem of accidental regularities*, so called because the theory seems to classify accidents such as (2) as laws. It is easy to generate other examples of this sort. Have a try yourself.[7]

Let's turn to a famous case that suggests that conditions (i)–(iv) are *unnecessary* for lawhood.

> All the fruit in Smith's garden at any time are apples. When one attempts to take an orange into the garden, it turns into an elephant. Bananas so treated become apples as they cross the boundary, while pears are resisted by a force that cannot be overcome. Cherry trees planted in the garden bear apples, or they bear nothing at all. If all these things were true, there would be a very strong case for its being a law that all the fruit in Smith's garden are apples. And this case would be in no way undermined if it were found that no other gardens, however similar to Smith's in all other respects, exhibited behavior of the sort just described. (Tooley, 1977, 686)

The expression "All the fruit in Smith's garden are apples" makes reference to Smith, so it violates condition (iv), according to which statements of laws must involve only nonlocal predicates. Nevertheless, it seems lawlike in Smith's world.[8]

---

[7] For more careful discussion of such objections, see Armstrong (1983, chap. 2).

[8] See Armstrong (1983, 26) for a less fanciful case and Lange (1995) and Dosanjh (2021) for further discussion of laws involving individuals.

The point of these examples is that our concept of *law* and our concept of *a regularity meeting conditions (i)–(iv)* seem to be different. As a result, the Naïve Regularity Theory does not capture our ordinary concept of law.

A comment on philosophical method: In describing these objections, I have appealed to intuitions, or the way that things seem, or to our ordinary way of thinking about the role of laws in science. This is standard practice in philosophy, though it remains controversial. I'll say more about these methodological issues in Sections 3 and 8, but for now I'll just mention two possible responses to these sorts of objections. One option is bite the bullet. A proponent of the Naïve Regularity Theory could simply accept that it *is* a law that all solid spheres of gold have radius < 1 km, and that there *could not be* any law involving Smith's garden. However, these are but two of many putative counterexamples (Armstrong, 1983, chap. 2), so applying this strategy across the board would require a radical revision to our concept of law. The more popular strategy is to revise the analysis of laws. Over the next few subsections, we'll examine a version of Humeanism that does a better job of classifying laws and accidents.

2.4 The Humean Best Systems Account

Here is a more popular account of how to analyze laws in terms of the Humean mosaic.

Humean Best Systems Account (BSA): Statements of laws are contingent generalizations in the best systematization of the Humean mosaic.

The best systematization of a mosaic is, roughly speaking, an efficient summary of its events. To make better sense of this, we need to clarify the concept of a *systematization* and we need to say something about which is *best*.

A *systematization* of a mosaic is just a set of sentences about that mosaic.[9] Consider a deterministic world in which Newton's laws hold. Suppose we provide a complete description of the world, point by point, analogous to a bitmap image file in which each pixel is assigned a color. We'll call this set of true singular sentences *HM*, short for 'Humean mosaic'. Now consider the set of all sentences entailed by *HM*.[10] This new set is the *deductive closure* of *HM*, so we'll label it *DC*. Now consider a set whose members are solely (*i*) statements describing the initial conditions and (*ii*) Newton's laws. We'll call this set *PL* after Pierre-Simon Laplace (1814/1999), who suggested that we imagine a god

---

[9] They are usually stipulated to be true sentences but not always (Braddon-Mitchell, 2001).

[10] Talk of one set entailing another is shorthand for saying that the members of one set entail the members of the other.

that specifies some initial conditions and dynamical laws and then lets nature run its course. *HM, DC*, and *PL* are *complete* systematizations of the Humean mosaic, which is to say that they entail all its facts. However, we may also construct *incomplete* systematizations. For example, consider a set consisting of (*i*) statements describing initial conditions and (*ii′*) some, but not all, of Newton's laws. We'll call this *PD* for 'partial description'.

Reflecting on our systematizations suggests some criteria for the *best* systematization. *HM, DC*, and *PL* are *stronger/more informative* than *PD*. *PD* and *PL* are *simpler* than *HM*, and *much* simpler than *DC*. (*DC* has the special honor of containing maximal redundancy.) Of the systematizations we have considered, *PL* has the best balance of the virtues of *simplicity* and *strength*. That's what makes it the best. *PL* is effectively an efficient lossless compression of all the information about the Humean mosaic.[11]

The canonical version of the BSA explicitly analyses lawhood in terms of these two virtues:

Mill/Ramsey/Lewis Best Systems Account: Statements of laws are contingent generalizations in the systematization of the Humean mosaic that best balances the virtues of *strength* and *simplicity* (Lewis, 1973; Mill, 1875/1987; Ramsey, 1978).[12]

We'll soon encounter a problem that demands refinement of this account, but first we'll consider some of its advantages.

2.5 Some Virtues of the Humean BSA

To begin, the BSA seems to retain most of the attractive features of the Naïve Regularity Theory. As a version of Humeanism, its ontology is economical and its conceptual primitives are easily grasped (but more on this in a moment). Moreover, like the Naïve Regularity Theory, the BSA seems to correctly classify paradigm statements of laws such as Schrödinger's equation. Schrödinger's equation provides an extremely accurate description of the behavior of quantum-mechanical systems, so it offers a tremendous amount of information content. Other things being equal, systematizations of our mosaic

---

[11] *Two unrelated notes:* First, I recommend Beebee's (2000, 574) discussion of "God's Big Book of Facts" to those who are struggling with the notion of a best systematization. Second, matters become more complicated when we incorporate chance (Lewis, 1994), but we'll ignore this for the sake of brevity.

[12] Attentive readers will notice that, although I've described some virtues associated with the best system, I haven't dispensed with 'best'. For an overview of debates about *which* virtues to use and how to *weight* them, see Eddon and Meacham's (2015) discussion of "the Metrics Question."

that include this generalization are likely to be stronger and simpler than systematizations that don't. Systematizations without Schrödinger's equation need to replace its information content with something else. Good luck finding a simpler way to do so.[13]

The Naïve Regularity Theory and the BSA are distinguished by their analyses of laws (and by the concepts required for these analyses). The BSA requires the concept of a best system and its corresponding virtues whereas the Naïve Regularity Theory does not. However, precisely because the BSA offers a different analysis of laws, it is better equipped to handle the extensional problems raised in the previous section.

Let's begin with the problem of accidental regularities. Recall statements (1) and (2):

(1) All solid spheres of uranium 235 have radius < 1 km.
(2) All solid spheres of gold have radius < 1 km.

Whereas (1) seems nomically necessary, (2) seems accidental. Both are lawlike according to the Naïve Regularity Theory but not according to the BSA. Suppose the best system consists of a description of initial conditions together with fundamental laws of particle physics (much like system *PL* discussed in Section 2.4). Removing any of these laws would result in a system that is a little simpler but much weaker. As it turns out, (1) is a straightforward consequence of the laws of particle physics. It holds even for systems in which initial conditions are very different – hence its nomic necessity. In contrast, (2) is not a consequence of the laws alone. Change the initial conditions without changing the laws and (2) might turn out to be false. Thus, (2) is accidental.[14]

As far as Smith's garden is concerned, there's nothing about the notion of a "systematization" that requires us to avoid reference to particulars. The BSA can accommodate the intuition that it could be a law that all the fruit in Smith's garden are apples. A system that includes this statement of law could completely describe the world while omitting a great many sentences describing particular matters of fact that would otherwise be required.

In sum, when it comes to classifying laws in accordance with our ordinary beliefs and scientific practices, the BSA does a better job than the Naïve Regularity Theory.

---

[13] This is not to say that it's impossible. This is the sort of thing that occurs with a scientific revolution or paradigm shift. Paradigm shifts involve a replacement of one theoretical system – i.e., a systematization – with another. This poses no problem for the BSA. Although our opinion of what the laws are changes in the course of a scientific revolution, the laws themselves don't.

[14] It should be noted that (2) *is* a consequence of our original best system – i.e., the laws *together with the initial conditions*. As a result, if we added (2) to our original system, the result would be a more complex system that is no stronger than the original.

2.6 Extensional Problems for the BSA

Although the BSA is a clear improvement on the Naïve Regularity Theory, philosophers have proposed some clever counterexamples. For example:

> Imagine a world containing ten different types of fundamental particles. Suppose further that the behavior of particles in interactions depends upon the types of the interacting particles. Considering only interactions involving two particles, there are 55 possibilities with respect to the types of the two particles. Suppose that 54 of these possible interactions have been carefully studied, with the result that 54 laws have been discovered, one for each case, which are not interrelated in any way. Suppose finally that the world is sufficiently deterministic that, given the way particles of types X and V are currently distributed, it is impossible for them ever to interact at any time, past, present, or future. (Tooley, 1977, 669)[15]

Could there be a law concerning XV interactions, even though there are no XV interactions? Tooley thinks so. However, the BSA cannot make sense of this possibility. There are no XV interactions to describe, and given the setup of the case there can be no unified theory of particle interactions, so *any* generalization concerning XV interactions would sacrifice simplicity without adding strength. Thus, the BSA entails that there cannot be an XV law in Tooley's scenario. This looks like an unfortunate consequence, since we seem to have no trouble imagining a possible world in which the XV law has some specific content even though it lacks instances.

In general, cases like Tooley's suggest that two worlds can agree on all particular matters of fact while containing different laws. But if laws reduce to regularities, as Humeanism claims, there can be no difference in laws without a difference in the Humean mosaic. Thus, it is hard to see how the BSA could be repaired to accommodate Tooley's possibilities. As a result, although the BSA has clear advantages over the Naïve Regularity Theory, it may not perfectly capture our ordinary notion of a law. However, sometimes philosophical reflection forces a revision of our ordinary concepts, and some Humeans are happy to bite the bullet (Beebee, 2000). (More on this in Section 3.)

2.7 A Puzzle Concerning the Language of Systematization

Let's consider another problem for the BSA raised by Lewis (1983, 367): some theoretical virtues are *language relative*. Consider our Newtonian world from Section 2.4. Introduce a new primitive predicate, F, that applies to all and only things in worlds in which system PL is true. The extremely simple sentence

---

[15] See Carroll (1994) and Maudlin (2007) for other influential counterexamples.

'Everything is *F*' entails *HM*. It is a complete systematization all on its own! And it is significantly simpler than our Newtonian systematization *PL*. Thus, it is possible to maximize both simplicity and strength by gerrymandering our predicates. However, doing so has unappealing consequences. To mention just one, the sentence 'Everything is *F*' strictly implies all truths; according to this systematization, *all* truths are natural necessities. The distinction between laws and accidents has been destroyed. As Lewis says, "That must be wrong" (Lewis, 1983, 367). Something seems amiss with predicate *F*. It feels like a philosopher's trick. No scientist would propose a theory involving gerrymandered predicates like that!

Therefore, in addition to describing some theoretical virtues that make one systematization better than another, we must specify which language to use when applying and weighting those virtues. There are, broadly speaking, two ways to deal with this problem.

2.7.1 Solution 1: Naturalness Constraints on Best Systems

Properties featured in science seem *natural*, whereas predicate *F* seems *nonnatural*. Let's illustrate this distinction with some examples. All objects with negative unit charge seem to be exactly similar in that crucial respect. This property is a candidate for a *perfectly natural property*. All green things are alike in color, but not exactly similar. *Green* is a candidate for a highly natural property. Let a *grue* object be one that is green and examined before time *t* or blue and unexamined before *t* (Goodman, 1955, 74). Intuitively, grue objects needn't be genuinely similar in color. *Grue* is less natural than *green*. Now consider a set of miscellaneous things – say, the set whose members are the number 2, Plato's beard, and your favorite song. There doesn't seem to be *any* genuine similarity among these objects; this property is as *nonnatural* as it gets. In sum, naturalness goes hand in hand with our notion of genuine similarity.[16]

The central claim here is that some ways of classifying objects are objectively better than others; only some classificatory schemes "carve nature at the joints" (Plato, *Phaedrus* 265d–266a). What is involved, metaphysically speaking, in accepting the distinction between natural and nonnatural properties? There are many options, but I'll mention just two. Some take naturalness as primitive (Sider, 2011). Everyone needs some primitives. And since we have a strong pretheoretical sense that there are objective similarities and differences in the world, this seems not to be terribly problematic. Others analyze naturalness in terms of *universals* (Armstrong, 1989a). Universals are fundamental

---

[16] For more on the natural/nonnatural distinction, see Lewis (1983), Armstrong (1989a), and Sider (2011). For a recent challenge, see Dasgupta (2018).

elements of an ontology that are posited to explain relations of similarity and difference among objects. Whenever two things are genuinely similar, that is because there is a *universal* – an entity that is wholly present in each of its instances – that the two things share (Armstrong, 1989a, esp. chap. 1). This approach takes our pretheoretical sense of genuine similarity and difference as a starting point for our metaphysical theorizing, but one that needs to be explained. In any case, the natural/nonnatural distinction requires some serious metaphysical machinery – some conceptual primitives that weren't invoked in our initial description of the Humean mosaic.

Let's return to predicate *F*. Why does it seem suspect? Well, consider any two of its instances. They don't need to be intrinsically similar *at all*. *F* looks like a predicate that has been gerrymandered with the specific purpose of creating a simple system. That misses the point of monadic predicates, which is to describe objective intrinsic similarities and differences among objects. This suggests a constraint on best systematizations: Don't appeal to gerrymandered, nonnatural properties! More carefully:

Naturalness Constraint: The best systematization must be expressed in a language whose predicates refer to perfectly natural properties.

The Naturalness Constraint allows us to ignore systematizations involving gerrymandered predicates like Lewis's *F* or gruesome predicates like Goodman's 'grue'. Thus, we have a metaphysical solution to a practical problem: we ought to use certain predicates rather than others because of the metaphysical structure of the world.

We'll now consider two influential types of objections to the Naturalness Constraint.

The first is a family of objections having to do with naturalness itself: *Is naturalness even intelligible? Can judgments of naturalness be made a priori? Are natural properties (or universals, or tropes, or . . .) parsimonious?*[17] The quick version of Lewis's response was to say that naturalness "was so commonsensical and so serviceable – indeed, was so often indispensable – that it was foolish to try to get on without it" (Lewis, 1999, 1–2). I won't attempt a careful assessment of these objections in this section, since we'll see that naturalness is required for many Non-Humean accounts of laws. I'll simply note that incorporating naturalness into a Humean account undermines part of the initial appeal

---

[17] Cowling (2017) provides a nice overview of these problems for abstract entities generally.

of Humeanism. It threatens to make the theory harder to understand and less economical.[18]

The second problem is related to the epistemology of laws: *Do judgments of naturalness feature in scientific practice?* We all agree that science is essential for the discovery of laws. However, if scientists don't make judgments of naturalness, the things they call "laws" might be different than the things considered to be laws by any theory employing the Naturalness Constraint. Consider this thought experiment:

> Suppose at a certain point in history, all the primitive scientific predicates are natural ones. Now suppose that one scientist devises a theory which is simpler and more informative than any to be had so far – but only by the use of new theoretical terms which do not stand for natural classes. Why should we think that his theory should be judged inferior? New theoretical terms are typically not definable in terms of the old, and on the other hand, are typically required for radical theoretical innovation. No, I expect that this would be the end of the natural classes' winning streak – the incorrect language would take over ... How could we designate this as an evil day for science? (van Fraassen, 1989, 53)

Van Fraassen is asking us to envision a scenario in which scientists violate the Naturalness Constraint. He suggests that there's nothing wrong with the violation. If that's right, it's possible for there to be a mismatch between our metaphysical account of laws (which *must* involve natural properties) and the laws discovered through the practice of actual science (which need *not* involve natural properties).[19]

This is an interesting objection, but it's not decisive. My own take (Hildebrand, 2019a) is that the mismatch objection rests on a conflation of two interpretations of the Naturalness Constraint. According to the weak interpretation, we should ignore systematizations that employ gruesome, gerrymandered predicates. Scientists do in fact follow that constraint, and it seems that, as van Fraassen envisions his case, his imagined scientists do as well. According to the strong interpretation, we should ignore any systematization employing a language with basic predicates that refer to anything other than the *actually instantiated* natural properties. That would require us to know which properties our world contained before engaging in scientific inquiry, violating the (obvious) fact that laws and properties are posited together as a package deal (Lewis, 1983; Loewer, 2007). However, proponents of the Naturalness Constraint do not require the strong interpretation.

---

[18] Eddon and Meacham (2015) cite many Humeans who express this worry.

[19] See Loewer (2007, 322) and Demarest (2017) for further discussion of this argument.

2.7.2 Solution 2: Pragmatic Constraints on Best Systems

Another response to the problem of Lewis's predicate F is to take a pragmatic, rather than metaphysical, turn: We should avoid predicates like F and *grue* in our scientific theorizing because doing so is in our *pragmatic interests*. For example, one important role of laws is to guide our predictions. If I know Newton's laws of motion, and I learn the masses and states of motion of various medium-sized objects (such as billiard balls on a table), I can predict their behavior with great accuracy.[20] Predicates like 'mass' and 'velocity' can help me find my way in the world. But predicate F cannot. To understand it, I would first need to learn *every* particular matter of fact. That I cannot do. And even if I could, as soon as I understood the predicate it would become useless for the purpose of making predictions. Or suppose that physicists are trying to fit a curve to some data. They realize that a highly gerrymandered piecewise function fits the data better than any smooth curve. Such functions are less useful for making novel predictions, so there's little point in working with them.

We can build the above insight into the BSA as follows:

Pragmatic Humeanism: Statements of laws are generalizations in the best systematization of the Humean mosaic, where the best systematization for a group is the one that is best suited to advance the interests of the group – for example, by producing useful predictions and explanations given the goals, abilities, and limitations of the group.[21]

Notice that this analysis is relativized to "groups". A god might be able to work with highly gerrymandered predicates such as F, but we can't. In answering the question "Which predicates should *we* use in *our* theorizing?," we have to attend to our own epistemic limitations and our own subjective interests.

Pragmatic Humeanism does not involve the additional metaphysical machinery of the Naturalness Constraint, which makes the view attractive to those who think that metaphysical posits are unhelpful in solving epistemological or practical problems. It preserves (or even enhances) the attractive features of Humeanism and the BSA – ontological economy, conceptual clarity, fit with scientific practice, etc. – without saddling us with new primitives.[22]

---

[20] Or, rather, Michael Tooley can – hence my losing record against him.

[21] For recent defenses of views in this vicinity, see Hall (2015), Dorst (2018), Hicks (2018), Jaag and Loew (2018), and Loewer (2021).

[22] In fact, I have doubts about this, because the concepts of *interests*, *abilities*, *limitations*, and *goals* do not strike me as metaphysically benign. But that's a project for another time.

However, there is an objection that arises with special force for Pragmatic Humeanism: It seems to imply that the laws of nature are *subjective*. That seems wrong.[23]

To evaluate this objection, we first need to understand the sort of subjectivism that Pragmatic Humeanism involves. It does *not* hold that *everything* is subjective. The Humean mosaic is objective. We do not, individually or collectively, have the power to change *that*. It is the laws that have an element of subjectivism. But they are not subjective in the following sense: Agents, either individually or collectively, can decide for themselves what the laws are. Rather, the laws are subjective only in the following weak sense: The features that determine which systematization of the mosaic is best are determined by our interests (by way of our epistemic abilities, limitations, and goals). To borrow from Jaag and Loew (2018), the best systematization is the one that is *best for us*. To some, even this limited sort of subjectivism might seem problematic.[24] However, Ned Hall suggests that this way of thinking implicitly assumes that *Humean* laws must have all the features of *Non-Humean* laws:

> It helps to keep firmly in mind that [Humeans think] that, for any world, *all there is* to that world is a distribution throughout space and time of various perfectly natural magnitudes. For example, all there is to our Newtonian particle world are some particles moving around, with masses and charges. That's it. It is emphatically *not* that the facts about these particles serve as clues to something "behind the scenes" that is directing their behavior. That is quite the wrong way to think about it. In fact, a much better way to think about the status of laws, given such a background metaphysics, is *pragmatically*. (Hall, 2015, 268)

When Hall talks about things lurking "behind the scenes," he's thinking about Non-Humean laws. Subjectivism about *Non-Humean* laws is, to my mind, utterly unintelligible.[25] That may explain why many of us, me included, are inclined to think that laws must be objective. But the fact that Non-Humean laws must be objective does not require Humean analyses of lawhood to be objective. If we make that assumption, we run the risk of simply begging the question against Humeanism. If statements of laws are just useful ways

---

[23] See Armstrong (1983, chap. 5) and Sánchez (in press). For other objections to Pragmatic Humeanism, see Friend (2022).

[24] Of course, the degree of subjectivism depends on how we interpret "us." Is it scientists, human beings, sentient beings, or what?

[25] Strictly speaking, I should say that subjectivism about Non-Humean *primitives* is unintelligible, since some Non-Humeans analyze laws in terms of more fundamental natural necessities. For example, Demarest (2017) and Kimpton-Nye (2017, 2021) propose a best systems analysis of laws while accepting a modally rich ontology of powers (a Non-Humean mosaic, if you will). They can endorse a degree of subjectivism about lawhood but not about fundamental powers.

of organizing information, there seems to be nothing wrong with interpreting usefulness in terms of our interests.

Thus, although I admit that it sounds strange to hold that lawhood is subjective, I think we should exercise caution in interpreting that as a serious objection to Pragmatic Humeanism.

2.8 Humeanism and Laws in the Special Sciences

Before closing, I'll mention one more extensional problem. The special sciences include statements of laws: for example, Mendel's Laws in biology and the Law of Demand in economics. These laws are used to make predictions and explanations, and thus seem to play a similar role in scientific practice as laws in fundamental physics – hence the label 'law'. However, their character is a bit different. Notably, they seem to admit of more exceptions, to be more contingent, and to exhibit less modal stability (i.e., to apply under a narrower range of background conditions). What can Humeans say about such laws?[26]

One position is that these so-called laws don't deserve their names. A generalization that has exceptions, is modally unstable, etc., is no law at all. If that's right, we shouldn't expect a metaphysical account of laws to classify these statements as laws. It should only apply to statements of laws in fundamental physics that (arguably) hold without exception.[27] This position may seem to suggest that philosophical analysis takes precedence over scientific practice, insofar as it requires us to reinterpret special science laws in other terms – e.g., in terms of "mechanisms" (Bechtel & Abrahamsen, 2005). For me, I don't see this as a serious cost, but some philosophers would prefer not to impose restrictions on the language used by scientists. They'd rather take scientific usage at face value.

Another option is to account for special science laws by reducing them to physical laws (plus background conditions). For example, we could try to make sense of the modal force of special science laws by paralleling the account of the modal force of statements (1) and (2) provided in Section 2.5. Perhaps we could articulate a gradable notion of *stability* tied to the range of background conditions under which a regularity holds and assign degrees of lawlikeness according to stability. If this strategy worked, the relevant reduction and relevant account of special science laws would be available to just about everyone

---

[26] For a general introduction to *ceteris paribus* laws and laws in the special sciences, see Reutlinger, Schurz, Hüttemann, and Jaag (2021).

[27] See Earman and Roberts (1999) for a general defense of this position. Cartwright (1999) and Kistler (2006) argue that laws should be given a unified treatment across scientific disciplines, with the accounts they provide pushing us in the direction of Non-Humeanism.

who accepts fundamental laws (including Non-Humeans). However, some philosophers of science are not optimistic about the prospects of reduction.[28]

Finally, suppose that special science laws are not reducible. In that case, some metaphysical accounts might accommodate them better than others. As Cohen and Callender (2009) point out, laws in the special sciences typically involve predicates that are less than perfectly natural. As a result, any theory with a Naturalness Constraint will struggle to classify them as laws. However, suppose that we allow ourselves flexibility concerning our choice of predicates and our choice of domains to systematize. We should systematize only those facts deemed directly relevant for a given special science when described in a language appropriate for that science; its generalizations will be laws of that science (Cohen & Callender, 2009; Schrenk, 2006, 2017). This choice of language and restriction of domain can be justified on pragmatic grounds, so this view seems to fit naturally with Pragmatic Humeanism.[29] If that's right, such accounts would accommodate scientific usage of the term 'law' at face value while avoiding the pitfalls of reductionism.

2.9 Conclusion

The BSA offers clear advantages over the Naïve Regularity Theory. However, there's still work to be done in clarifying the costs associated with the Naturalness Constraint and with various forms of Pragmatic Humeanism. Now that we have a better sense of how Humeanism works, we can turn our attention to some problems that (supposedly) hold for all versions of Humeanism.

3 Objections to Humeanism

Suppose that some version of Humeanism is *extensionally adequate* – that is, that it does a satisfactory job of classifying statements as laws or accidents. Even so, Humean laws might not have all the properties laws should have. Laws that reduce to regularities might be incapable of playing certain roles we want laws to play. In other words, Humeanism might struggle to satisfy various *intensional criteria* for a theory of laws. In this section, we'll consider objections of this sort.

It will sometimes be helpful to present these objections in terms of the following argument schema:

---

[28] For an argument that Lewis's version of the BSA *cannot* accommodate special science laws, see Cohen and Callender (2009). Tahko (2021) includes a useful overview of influential challenges to attempts to reduce special sciences to physics.

[29] In addition to those just cited, see Mitchell (2000) for a pragmatist approach to special science laws.

(1) Laws _____ .

(2) If Humeanism is true, it's not the case that laws _____ .

(3) Therefore, Humeanism is false.

However, the objections don't need to be interpreted as having such strong conclusions. While a theory's inability to satisfy a certain criterion is a mark against it, contrary to what the above schema suggests, it may not be decisive. It might turn out that *no* theory of laws satisfies all our criteria.

3.1 Laws govern

We often speak of laws "governing" nature, in somewhat the same manner as political laws govern societies. Both sorts of laws impose structure on the world by constraining and restricting the course of events. In the history of philosophy, it was common to take the notion of governance literally and hold that laws of nature require "lawgivers" just as much as political laws. For example, here's St. Thomas Aquinas:

> So the world is governed through the providence of that intellect that gave to nature this order, and we may compare the providence through which God governs the world to the domestic foresight through which a man governs his family or to the political foresight through which a ruler governs a city or land, directing the actions of others towards a definite end with respect to himself. (Aquinas, 1972, q.5, a.2, 189)[30]

Here's Descartes, speaking about laws of mathematics:

> [I]t is God who has laid down these laws in nature just as a king lays down laws in his kingdom. (Descartes, 1984, AT I 145, 23)

In his *Principles of Philosophy*, Descartes makes similar claims about God's relationship to the laws of nature, but the analogy is less explicit.[31] And here's Isaac Newton, in the "General Scholium" to his *Principia*:

> This most elegant system of the sun, planets, and comets could not have arisen without the design and dominion of an intelligent and powerful being. (Newton, 2014, 111)

These thinkers take the governing metaphor at face value: God is the author of the laws of nature and is thus ultimately responsible for imposing regularities on nature. (We'll consider their account of laws in the next section.) However, one

---

[30] See Hattab (2018) for further discussion of the relationship between Aquinas's conception of law and the conception of governing law in early modern philosophy, and see Ott (2009) for an accessible overview of early modern thought concerning laws (in which the notion of governance plays a very important role).

[31] See Ott and Patton (2018) for further discussion.

can embrace the notion of governance in a less literal sense without appealing to a personal being. The idea would be that although there isn't *someone* imposing structure on nature, *something* does – and we call these somethings "laws of nature".

The claim that laws govern is controversial, but it does seem to map pretty naturally to the way we speak about laws. This suggests the following argument:

(1_G) Laws govern.
(2_G) If Humeanism is true, it's not the case that laws govern.
(3)   Therefore, Humeanism is false.

Is this bad news for Humeanism? Maybe not. The interpretation of governance sketched here – in which a governing law imposes structure on nature in the way that a god might impose structure on nature – entails Non-Humeanism. So interpreted, (1_G) is simply a way of saying that Humeanism is false! However, if we opt for a weaker interpretation of governance, then (2_G) might be false. Suppose one says:

> Look, all this talk of gods or governors imposing structure is just a fanciful way to say that laws feature in explanations. But Humeans can give an account of how laws explain (see discussion in Section 3.3), so that means that they can also affirm the sentence "laws govern" when it is interpreted appropriately.[32]

If that's right, it will be hard to defend this objection to Humeanism.

A more modest appeal to governance might work as follows. Governance is a criterion for a theory of laws, but not an important one. The fact that Humean laws don't govern is merely a strike against them. It isn't decisive, though it might play some role in our ultimate accounting of pros and cons.

Even this more modest approach is controversial. It's important to attend to historical context when appealing to intuitions and ordinary concepts. As the discussion in this subsection suggests, the concept of law featured in early modern science was frequently connected to a Non-Humean view according to which nature is literally governed by God. I don't wish to overstate the connection (see Ruby, 1986), but it seems sufficiently strong that our intellectual history may incline us to speak as though laws govern. However, we aren't committed to all the positions of our ancestors. Given this context, the intuitive appeal of the notion that laws govern might count for nothing at all (Beebee, 2000; Loewer, 1996; Ott & Patton, 2018).

---

[32] These words are mine, but see Roberts (2008) for a defense of this sort of position.

This might seem obvious. However, it's important to understand the response to the governance objection, because other objections to Humeanism may involve implicit appeals to the idea that laws govern. Here are two potential examples.

Armstrong (1983, 39–40) argues that Humeanism fails to explain the "inner connection" between multiple instances of the same law. Suppose it is a law that all Fs are Gs. Why, then, is some particular F a G? Because of the law, surely. But, for Humeans, this explanation amounts to saying something like: "This particular F is a G because the first F is G, the second F is G, ..., the nth F is G, and there are no other Fs." That doesn't seem to capture the sort of connection we have in mind; nowhere does it involve the idea that this particular object's being F is what *makes* it a G. This is an interesting objection, but the claim that laws involve an inner connection sounds a lot like the claim that laws govern.

In the previous section, we encountered Tooley's ten-particle case. There are many related cases that suggest that the Humean mosaic does not suffice to determine the laws. Here's an example:

> Consider, for example, a world in which there is only one particle, which happens to instantiate mass. Such a particle will behave inertially for all time. Therefore, according to the BSA, there is one law at this world: all massive particles travel inertially for all time. But, intuitively, the law should say that massive particles attract other massive particles and behave inertially only in the absence of other massive particles. (Demarest, 2017, 43)

Why should we think that the nomic structure of this world is more complex than the BSA would suggest? Let's imagine a series of worlds. Begin with a large Newtonian world in which it is a law that massive particles attract other massive particles and behave inertially only in the absence of other massive particles. The next world in the series is just a bit smaller, but it has the same laws. The next world is even smaller. And so on. Demarest is simply asking us to consider the limiting case of this series. It seems like laws should be distinguished from initial conditions, and laws aren't vague, so the fact that one world is a bit smaller than the next shouldn't make a difference to the laws.[33]

Intuitively, this seems correct. But it may seem correct because we're tacitly assuming that laws govern. And similarly for Tooley's ten-particle case. It seems possible that there could be an XV law, but that may be because we implicitly assume that laws stand apart from nature and govern.

The bottom line: Appeals to some sort of governance criterion have been influential, but I'm not sure they count for much. Accommodating governance

---

[33] See Chen (in press) for a challenge to the distinction between laws and initial conditions.

is, at best, one criterion among many – and arguably one that shouldn't have much weight. We should exercise caution when appealing to our ordinary concepts and intuitions concerning laws, especially as far as the notion of governance is concerned.

3.2 Laws Support Counterfactuals

As our discussion in Section 3.1 suggests, we ordinarily think that laws are supposed to do some heavy lifting. They make things happen! As a result, they're also relevant to what would happen in various situations, even if those situations aren't actually realized. This is to say that laws play an important role in providing the truth conditions for subjunctive conditionals. *Counterfactual conditionals* are an especially vexing sort of subjunctive: They are if-then statements in which the antecedent is never realized, which makes it particularly difficult to explain their truth conditions.

For example, my first smartphone never broke, though it had no case and no screen protector. (I lived dangerously before having children.) Nevertheless, the following sentence seems true: "If I had dropped my phone from the fourth story to the concrete sidewalk below, it would have broken." The antecedent of the conditional is contrary to fact. Why, then, are we confident that my phone would have broken? We imagine a world, call it w_1, very much like ours up to a certain point in time. We then suppose that I drop my phone in w_1. We appeal to the laws of nature, which we stipulate to be the same as the laws in the actual world, to deduce what happens next: my phone breaks.

This makes a lot of sense for Non-Humeans. Their laws (or natural necessities) are prior to the distribution of events in the mosaic and impose structure on it. However, it's less clear that this procedure is available to Humeans. After all, they take the Humean mosaic to be prior to the laws. It is puzzling why we should hold fixed something that is *nonfundamental* (the laws) and use it to say what would have happened at the *fundamental level* (events in the mosaic). A Humean mosaic ultimately consists of one little thing and then another, where each is, metaphysically speaking, entirely independent of everything else. So why should Humeans think that events in w_1 are relevant to what would have happened *in the actual world*? Humean laws don't *do* anything, so why not some other world instead? For example, consider w_2, a world in which the Humean mosaic is the same as w_1 up to and including the dropping of my phone, but in which my phone lands on the concrete unscathed; or consider w_3, which is like w_1 and w_2 but in which my phone accelerates away from the earth's center instead of towards it; or w_4, … well, you get the idea. Each of these worlds consists of a perfectly legitimate Humean mosaic. Each shares our world's history up to the time at which the phone is dropped. What makes w_1 special?

Humeans usually respond by *stipulating* that sameness of (Humean) laws is relevant. Then they use the procedure described immediately above.[34] As a result, they can provide a semantics for counterfactuals that provides intuitively correct truth-values for counterfactual sentences. However, there remains a difference between the Humean and Non-Humean accounts. Whereas everyone needs to say that we ought to hold the laws fixed when determining which worlds are relevant to the evaluation of counterfactuals, only Non-Humeans can provide an *explanation* of why this is so. By their lights, the laws are, in some sense, metaphysically prior to and determinative of regularities. The regularities occur because of the laws in a robust metaphysical sense. Humeans have no analogous story to tell. Their only recourse is to stipulate that laws are held fixed. This is not to say that they cannot motivate this stipulation. After all, it aligns with how we operate when using laws to give explanations, make predictions, and support counterfactuals, and our practices certainly seem to work. However, motivating the stipulation is not the same as explaining it in terms of the underlying metaphysics.[35]

Speaking for myself, I think this looks like a serious shortcoming for Humeanism. But we have to be careful. The claim that one must be able to explain why laws should be held fixed might turn out to be similar to the claim that an adequate theory of laws must *govern* nature and *explain* regularities in the metaphysical sense distinctive of Non-Humean theories. Our examination of counterfactuals may simply illustrate another way in which Humeanism requires a revision to our ordinary concept of laws.

3.3 Laws Explain Regularities and/or Their Instances

Explanatory considerations feature in different sorts of objections to Humeanism. In Section 7, we'll consider an argument that some Non-Humean theory provides the best explanation of regularities. In this subsection, we'll examine an argument that Humeanism involves an explanatory circularity.

Here is the objection in a nutshell. According to Humeanism, the Humean mosaic is prior to laws; the laws are what they are because the mosaic is the way it is. Thus, regularities explain laws. However, in scientific practice laws are posited *to explain* regularities. As a result, Humeanism appears to be committed

---

[34] See Lewis (1973).

[35] See Maudlin (2007) for a careful defense of this objection. For a response along Pragmatic Humean lines, see Dorst (2022).

to an explanatory circle: the regularities explain the laws which explain the regularities. This is problematic because nothing explains itself.[36]

Let's consider how this argument fits the general schema:

(1_E) Laws explain.

(2_E) If Humeanism is true, it's not the case that laws explain (because laws are explained by the mosaic).

(3) Therefore, Humeanism is false.

The crucial issue is how *explanation* is to be interpreted. Loewer (1996) suggests a distinction between scientific and metaphysical explanation, and he argues that the premises are true only when interpreted as follows:

(1_{ES}) Laws explain *scientifically* – specifically, they explain by unifying, insofar as they present information in a deductive system whose axioms can be used as general premises in scientific explanations.

(2_{EM}) If Humeanism is true, it's not the case that laws *metaphysically* explain (because laws are metaphysically explained by the mosaic).

(3) Therefore, Humeanism is false.

This version of the argument is invalid, since premises (1_{ES}) and (2_{EM}) appeal to different sorts of explanation.

This topic has received lots of recent attention.[37] Much of the discussion concerns bridge principles that link scientific and metaphysical explanation.[38] Some of the discussion concerns whether Humeans should modify their account of the relationship between laws and the mosaic – for example, by holding that the mosaic doesn't explain the laws in the first place[39] or by holding that laws feature in higher-order explanations of facts in the mosaic.[40] There are interesting questions about how exactly Humeans should interpret explanatory claims, but unfortunately we don't have the space to examine them.

However, we can draw an interesting conclusion even without settling these debates. The above summary, brief as it is, suggests a familiar takeaway. No version of the explanatory circularity argument will be rhetorically effective *if* one assumes that laws must explain *by governing*.[41] If you assume that, of

---

[36] See Armstrong (1983, 4) and Maudlin (2007, 172) for influential statements of this objection.

[37] Bhogal (2020a, 2–3) provides a nice overview.

[38] See, for example, Lange (2013, 2018), Hicks and van Elswyk (2015), Miller (2015), Emery (2019), Shumener (2019), and Bhogal (2020b).

[39] See, for example, Miller (2015, section 3) and Kovacs (2020). I must profess some doubts about whether such views preserve the spirit of Humeanism.

[40] See Hicks (2021) and Skow (2016).

[41] I should clarify that I do not take the assumption that laws govern to be an essential feature of explanatory circularity arguments. Other concepts of explanation might lead to circularity as well! See, for example, Shumener (2019).

course you'll think that Humeanism runs into a circularity. But Humeans don't accept that assumption. Presumably we should grant them at least some leeway in interpreting the concept of explanation. Once again, this may involve a revision of our ordinary way of thinking about the role of laws in explanations. That isn't necessarily a decisive mark against Humeanism.

3.4 Laws Support Induction

In addition to supporting counterfactuals and explanations, laws support *predictions*. Thus, laws of nature are relevant to philosophical problems pertaining to *induction*: the form of inference in which we project patterns from the observed to the unobserved. There are two main philosophical problems pertaining to induction. We'll begin with a brief summary of both.

First, consider the inference below:[42]

Copper: In the past, all pieces of copper have expanded when heated; therefore, the next piece of copper will expand when heated.

It is not immediately obvious why the premise supports the conclusion, since we can imagine scenarios in which the premise is true and the conclusion is false. We'd like an intermediate premise that illuminates the connection. The obvious candidate is the principle *that nature is uniform*. Unfortunately, the original problem has been replaced with one just as difficult: Why think that nature is uniform? The uniformity of nature can't be established a priori, for that's simply not how we learn about the natural world. Neither can it be established a posteriori, for that appears to require a circular use of induction itself – for example, by appealing to the fact that observed parts of nature have been uniform hitherto. Either way, induction cannot be justified. *The problem of induction* is the problem of explaining why we ought to trust any inductive inferences at all in light of this skeptical argument.[43]

Second, consider the following inference – one that has the same logical form as the inference about copper.

Third Sons: In the past, all men in this room have been third sons; therefore, the next man to enter this room will be a third son.

This inference does not seem inductively valid. In general, the quality of an inductive inference is not determined by its logical form alone but also by some of its semantic features – such as the predicates it involves or whether

---

[42] The cases are borrowed from Goodman (1955).
[43] The skeptical argument is due to Hume (1748/2000, section 4).

the regularity it involves is lawlike or accidental. It would be nice to have an account of the distinction between good and bad inductive inferences. I'll call this *the problem of projection*.[44]

So much for background. How are these problems relevant to Humeanism? In short, Humeanism seems to render the problem of induction insoluble. This would be a bitter pill to swallow, for it would seem to undermine the epistemic foundations of the natural sciences. Why might Humeans have special difficulties in justifying induction? Consider the Humean account of nature: It consists of a mosaic of particular matters of fact, none of which stand in any necessary connections to one another. Because all events are "loose and separate," as Hume put it (*Enquiry*, section 7), there is an enormous range of future possibilities consistent with the actual past. Suppose I have just dropped my phone from the fourth story. What should we predict? In Section 3.2, we considered some worlds with the same history up to the dropping of the phone, at which point:

w_1: my phone breaks.
w_2: my phone lands unscathed.
w_3: my phone accelerates upward.

There are, of course, countless others. From the Humean perspective, why should we think that we're in w_1 as opposed to the others? Nothing guides the course of events. Nothing makes my phone break. It just happens (if it happens at all). There's no hope of finding an a priori reason to prefer one world to another, and appealing to past regularities leads to hopeless circularity. As a result, Humeans seem powerless to push back against Hume's skeptical argument.[45]

How should Humeans respond? A common response is that *no one* can justify induction.[46] A problem for all is a problem for none. The only rational response to a universal problem is to make our peace with the problem and move on.

Here's how a Humean might make peace with the problem. Consider the practice of scientific theorizing. Scientists simply *assume* that there are timeless regularities in nature waiting to be discovered. Like everyone else, they

---

[44] This, too, is an old problem, but for a careful formulation see Goodman (1955).

[45] See Armstrong (1983), Fales (1990), and Foster (2004) for defenses of this argument. Recently, some philosophers have argued that matters are even worse. For example, Segal (2020) argues that Humeans are committed to the conclusion that inductive inferences are *irrational* – that we should not make them at all.

[46] See, for example, Loewer (1996) and Beebee (2011). For my take in defense of Non-Humean justifications of induction, see Hildebrand (2018).

believe this on the basis of instinct, as Hume (1748/2000, section 5) suggests. So suppose we take the uniformity of nature for granted. (Of course, such an assumption does not *epistemically justify* the belief.) Well, once we grant that there *are* timeless regularities – something that Humeans are happy to do – we don't need to solve the problem of induction in order to make progress with the problem of projection. Take the BSA, for instance. It suggests a nice account of why lawlike regularities are better suited for projection than other regularities. Because they're axioms in the best systematization of particular matters of fact, they're more stable and more resilient than other sorts of regularities. We're less prone to inductive errors when we rely on these sorts of regularities. Many details need to be filled in, of course, but one can see how this has the potential to be an attractive view.[47]

If that's right, Humeans *can* claim that laws are relevant to induction and that laws *do* play a significant role in "supporting" inductive inferences: Without the notion of a law, we can't make useful distinctions between the good and bad inductive inferences![48] That's pretty significant. As with the other criteria we have discussed, this may involve a reinterpretation of the role of laws in "supporting induction," since they can't *justify* the practice itself.

3.5 Conclusion

To this point, we've seen that Humeanism has some attractive features but that it is susceptible to a number of objections. Unfortunately, we're not yet in the position to evaluate these objections. There are a few reasons for this.

First, it remains to be seen if the details of any Humean account can be spelled out in detail. For example, as noted in Section 2.1, I haven't said much about how we should characterize the Humean mosaic.

Second, I haven't said much about how Humean accounts of laws might fit into our broader metaphysics. For example, I haven't said anything about how Humeans might try to make sense of the notion of *chance*, which has important connections to probabilistic laws.[49]

Third, we've seen that Humeans have interesting responses to the objections considered in this section. Often, this involves reinterpretations of the

---

[47] Disclaimer: I haven't introduced "gruesome" predicates in this discussion, but doing so might make the problem of projection more difficult. It might even require something like the Naturalness Constraint.

[48] Goodman (1955) notes the connection between projectibility and lawlikeness but spends little time discussing laws. I've framed the solution as involving the BSA rather than Goodman's notion of "entrenched predicates," because Goodman's solution involves an element of subjectivism that Humeans are not required to accept.

[49] See, for example, Lewis (1994), Hall (2004), Briggs (2009), and Emery (2017).

operative criteria, which requires some revision to our ordinary concepts. One might worry that the quantity of reinterpretations is problematic, but the criteria in this section are not independent. There are deep connections among them. If that's right, it is to be expected that there might be a unified response to the sorts of objections considered here.[50]

Here, then, is my take on where we stand. Humeanism has some attractive features: its conceptual machinery seems easy enough to understand, its ontology is sparse, and some Humean analyses of laws have the potential to align nicely with scientific practice and to accommodate many of our intuitions about laws. One can see why Humeanism appeals to those with an inclination towards minimalistic metaphysics. However, it does require some revisions to our ordinary way of thinking about laws.

For me, I find some of these revisions disappointing. When I first started asking philosophical questions about the nature of laws, I wanted to accommodate ordinary intuitions and scientific practice at face value – or close to it. More importantly, I hoped to discover an explanation of why scientific methods are some of the best methods we have for learning about nature. It's not clear that Humeanism can deliver. Thus, although the objections we have considered are far from decisive, I think they are strong enough to motivate the search for a competing theory. Once we've explored some competing views, we'll be in a better position to evaluate these arguments and consider others as well.

4 Non-Humean Theories of Laws

4.1 Introduction

It's time to consider Non-Humeanism more carefully. Here's an abbreviated statement of the view.

Non-Humeanism: The world is like a grand mosaic, but it's *not* the case that its tiles could have been arranged any which way. Something imposes structure on it, analogously to the way in which the computer program *Virtual Physicists* imposes structure on its virtual environments. In other words, there is some sort of basic, fundamental necessity: something that governs, produces, or somehow constrains patterns of events in nature.

Why might Non-Humeanism be attractive? For starters, it has an easier time accommodating some of the criteria for a theory of laws that were introduced in previous sections.

---

[50] Bhogal (2020b) argues that Humeans require a distinctive sense of explanation – one that differs from our ordinary concept. Once articulated, this concept suggests a unified response to many of these objections.

On the surface, Non-Humeanism seems well-equipped to avoid the problems of extensional adequacy that beset Humeanism. For example, consider putative failures of supervenience such as Demarest's single particle case or Tooley's ten-particle world. Since Non-Humean laws are prior to regularities, there's no problem with positing distinct worlds with the same particular matters of fact but different laws.

Similarly, Non-Humeanism seems well-equipped to satisfy intensional criteria for a theory of laws. Do Non-Humean laws govern? Well, the primitives posited by Non-Humeans – God, fundamental dispositions, primitive laws, etc. – impose structure on nature, which seems analogous to the way in which political laws impose structure on society. Does Non-Humeanism support counterfactuals? As noted in Section 3.2, it appears so precisely because Non-Humean primitive necessities are prior to regularities in the mosaic. Do Non-Humean laws explain? Sure, for similar reasons, and they seem to have no problem avoiding circularity. Do Non-Humean laws support induction? According to Non-Humeanism, there's an explanation for regularities we have observed so far. But Non-Humean primitives – God, relations between universals, primitive laws that stand outside space and time, etc. – don't seem to be the sorts of things that can change with time. As a result, believing in such entities at least seems relevant to whether we're justified in believing that nature is uniform.

Obviously, there's a lot of controversial material packed into the two paragraphs above. However, on the surface, Non-Humeanism seems well-suited towards the satisfaction of these sorts of criteria. Thus, although positing modally robust primitives is costly, Non-Humeanism promises a nice return on this investment.

In later sections, we'll take a closer look at whether Non-Humeans can make good on these sorts of promises. In the remainder of this section, we'll introduce four of the most influential versions of Non-Humeanism and provide a general taxonomy of Non-Humean theories.

4.2 Four Important Theories

4.2.1 Divine Voluntarism

To begin, I'll describe a version of Non-Humeanism that takes the governing metaphor from Section 3 at face value: a *person*, God, authors and enforces the laws of nature. More precisely:

Divine Voluntarism: There is an intelligent being, God, that has the power to intentionally control the distribution of events in our world – that is, to determine whether there are regularities or not. Statements of laws describe the regularities supported by God's general decrees.[51]

This view is less popular than it once was, but it provides a natural starting point for our examination of Non-Humean theories. For starters, it was the received view during the early modern period (Ott, 2009; Ott & Patton, 2018; Psillos, 2018), and it is the account of laws suggested in Newton's "General Scholium" to his *Principia Mathematica* (2014, 109–114). For this reason, it has probably been influential in shaping our concept of laws. In addition, the concept of of God is relatively familiar. You probably have some idea of the Western theological/philosophical concept of God even if other staples of Non-Humean metaphysics – natural kind essences, platonic universals, etc. – are foreign to you.

As far as metaphysical machinery is concerned, the most obvious difference between Divine Voluntarism and Humeanism is that Divine Voluntarism posits a powerful person, God. Thus, its ontology is larger than that of Humeanism. But God is not merely another individual; God is special. In order to describe God, we require some new predicates – and thus we require some new conceptual resources – that aren't required to describe the Humean mosaic.

Let's clarify these conceptual resources. Why does Divine Voluntarism constitute a version of Non-Humeanism? Well, according to our definition, God is *powerful*. Here's one way to make this concept more precise:

Omnipotence Axiom: God is the being such that, *necessarily*, for all statements p, $\ulcorner$God wills that $p\urcorner$ entails p.[52]

In other words, this axiom says that God is so powerful that God gets what God wants, no matter what.[53] This axiom violates Humeanism, because it involves a primitive, unanalyzable necessity. (If you're worried about the intelligibility of this concept, stay tuned. That is the topic of Section 5.)

It should be noted that there are options for interpreting God's power and for interpreting modally robust primitives generally speaking. These result in

---

[51] This is an elaboration on the definition presented in (Hildebrand & Metcalf, 2022, 4). See Foster (2004), Swinburne (2006), and Collins (2009) for other contemporary defenses. Some Divine Voluntarists say more about God – for example, that God is benevolent – but our definition doesn't include such claims.

[52] Logicians don't like putting variables within quotes. We don't want the axiom to say that God wills a variable! It should say that God's will pertains to the contents of whatever sentence is substituted in place of the variable. The odd-looking corner brackets are a logician's shorthand for that.

[53] This axiom may require clarification or amendment to avoid paradoxes such as the paradox of the stone (Hoffman & Rosenkrantz, 2022), but for our purposes we can ignore such complications.

different flavors of Divine Voluntarism. The axiom above employs regular old metaphysical necessity. However, we could instead take the notion of *power* as primitive; we could introduce a primitive notion of *essence* to characterize God; we could speak of nature's *dependence* on God; we could posit a primitive relation of *chance* that obtains between God's will and the course of nature; and so on.[54]

To close, I'll make a final clarification. Like Humeanism, Divine Voluntarism does *not* treat the concept of law as fundamental. In saying that laws are regularities supported by divine decrees, Divine Voluntarism offers an analysis of lawhood in terms of its more fundamental concepts.

4.2.2 Primitivism

Let's turn to another, increasingly popular version of Non-Humeanism.

Primitivism: Laws are primitives. Like God, they are distinct from nature and impose structure on nature. However, they aren't persons, nor do they involve persons.[55]

If asked to clarify how a primitive law imposes structure on nature, Primitivists can offer an axiom such as this:

Axiom for Primitive Laws: The locution 'it is a law that' functions as a modal operator axiomatized as follows: necessarily, for all statements p, ⌐it is a law that p⌐ entails p. A primitive law, then, is just a primitive entity that makes the statement of law true.[56]

Notice that this axiom is similar to the Omnipotence Axiom discussed in Section 4.2.1. If we understand one, presumably we understand the other. The major difference is that primitive laws aren't personal. As with Divine Voluntarism, there are many options for how we axiomatize primitive laws, involving different sorts of modally robust primitives.

Primitivism is unique among Non-Humean theories in a crucial respect: For Primitivism, laws are part of the fundamental ontology, and the concept of a

---

[54] The differences here are subtle, and we don't have the space to examine them. Koslicki (2013), Raven (2015), and McKenzie (2022) provide nice points of entry into the literature on "post-modal" metaphysics. For discussions of the modal character of Non-Humeanism specifically, see Schrenk (2010), Wilsch (2021), Emery (2019), Hildebrand (2020c), and Shumener (in press).

[55] For defenses of Primitivism or closely related views, see Carroll (1994), Maudlin (2007), Kment (2014), and Chen and Goldstein (2022).

[56] If Primitivists allow truths without truthmakers, primitive laws needn't be entities at all. They could simply be the primitive modal truths themselves.

law is simply primitive. All others analyze the concept of law in terms of other primitives.

4.2.3 DTA: External Relations between Universals

When we examine the concept of law featured in modern science, the above accounts seem to leave something out: Laws explain the behavior of objects in virtue of their *properties*. For example, the 'F', 'm', and 'a' in $F = ma$ (Newton's second law) refer to properties of objects. Maybe laws are *modal relations among properties*?

According to Dretske (1977), Tooley (1977), and Armstrong (1983), laws of nature are higher-order states of affairs.[57] They consist of a nomic relation holding between first-order universals. As discussed in Section 2.7, universals are posited to ground natural properties (Armstrong, 1989a). Nomic relations themselves have four crucial features. They are *second-order:* Their relata are universals, not particulars. They are *external:* They do not hold solely in virtue of their relata. They are *irreducible:* Nomic relations are fundamental universals themselves, so whether a nomic relation binds two universals cannot be reduced to other features of the world, including facts about which natural regularities occur. Finally, they are *modally laden.* For example, consider the following axiom:

Nomic Necessitation Axiom: The relation of *nomic necessitation (N)* is the unique irreducible relation such that, necessarily, for any two universals F and G, if F and G stand in the relation $N(F, G)$ then all Fs are Gs.

As is common, let's call the theory that laws are second-order relations between universals *DTA*, after Dretske, Tooley, and Armstrong. Their laws play the same governing role as primitive laws, but the governing entities posited by DTA have an internal metaphysical structure.

The ontology of DTA may be more complex than that of Primitivism. Notably, Primitivism seems to be compatible with nominalism about properties, whereas DTA requires universals.[58] Thus, like Divine Voluntarism, DTA requires an analysis of laws in terms of its primitives. As far as modally robust primitives are concerned, DTA has much in common with Primitivism and

---

[57] My overview of this theory is borrowed from Hildebrand (2020c, 367) and Hildebrand (2020b, 3).

[58] Carroll (1994), a primitivist, accepts nominalism. Maudlin (2007), another primitivist, accepts universals, but they are not incorporated into his analysis of laws. Armstrong and Tooley disagree about how many nomic relations there are and whether universals are immanent or transcendent. See Hildebrand (2020c) for an argument that DTA requires transcendent universals.

Divine Voluntarism: Primitive modality is incorporated into the theories in different ways, but the modality itself is similar across the theories. This is apparent in the three axioms we have considered. These differences may seem subtle, but we'll see later that they are important.

4.2.4 Dispositionalism

We'll now consider a related view: *Dispositionalism.*[59] Like DTA, properties play a prominent role in this account of laws (or of nomic necessity). However, the nature of properties is different. Here is Alexander Bird's sketch of the view:

> [L]aws are not thrust upon properties, irrespective, as it were, of what those properties are. Rather the laws spring from within the properties themselves. The essential nature of a property is given by its relations with other properties. (Bird, 2007, 2)

Consider the property *mass*. According to DTA, objects with mass exhibit certain kinds of behavior because a nomic relation involving the property of mass happens to obtain; had a different nomic relation obtained, massive objects would have behaved differently. But, according to Dispositionalism, the behavior of massive objects flows from the very nature of mass itself. The modal relations between properties are not imposed "from the outside" by external, contingent relations; rather, the relations are (speaking loosely) *constitutive* of the properties.

To make the example more precise, suppose Dispositionalists posit a property of Newtonian gravitational mass axiomatized as follows:

Mass Axiom: *Newtonian gravitational mass* is the unique property such that, necessarily, any two massive objects experience an attractive force inversely proportional to the square of their distances (described precisely by Newton's Law of Universal Gravitation).

This seems intelligible insofar as the embedded necessity operator is intelligible. As with other Non-Humean theories, axioms needn't use regular old metaphysical necessity; a different modally robust primitive could be used instead – perhaps even dispositionality itself (Anjum & Mumford, 2018).

However we axiomatize fundamental dispositions, the ontology of Dispositionalism differs radically from that of Humeanism. Dispositionalism reinterprets all of nature, treating fundamental facts in the mosaic as modally-rich. Figure 1 illustrates the difference between Humeanism, a

---

[59] Proponents include Shoemaker (1980), Swoyer (1982), Cartwright (1999), Heil (2003), Molnar (2003), Mumford (2004), Bird (2007), Chakravartty (2007), Tugby (2013b), Tugby (2013a), Demarest (2017), and Williams (2019).

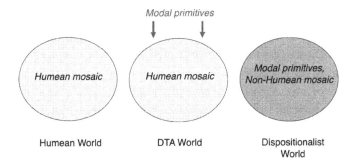

Figure 1 Where are the modal primitives?

standard version of DTA, and Dispositionalism. Humeanism posits no modal primitives. DTA is compatible with treating nature as a Humean mosaic, in which structure is imposed from the outside. Dispositionalism builds primitive modality into the mosaic itself. It does so by individuating properties by their modal relations to other properties.[60]

Let's take a closer look at Dispositionalism's metaphysical machinery. To begin, why is it called 'Dispositionalism'? The idea, in short, is that it's built into the nature of a property that its instances are disposed towards certain kinds of behaviors. For example, to have mass is (in part) to be disposed to attractive forces towards other massive objects. But in certain impoverished worlds, such as Demarest's example of the single particle world mentioned in Section 3.1, being disposed towards some behavior doesn't entail that behavior. There is flexibility concerning the nature of dispositions we posit. We can allow spontaneously manifesting dispositions, dispositions whose manifestations are probabilistic, and so on.[61]

Interestingly, whereas DTA seems to require universals, Dispositionalism seems to be compatible with different views about the nature of natural properties. Some treat properties as transcendent universals capable of uninstantiated existence (Bird, 2007; Tugby, 2013b), whereas others treat them as worldly tropes – i.e., as concrete particulars rather than abstract universals (Coates, 2022; Heil, 2003). Some have even proposed nominalistic versions of

---

[60] In the metaphysics of property individuation there is an important debate between Dispositionalism's account of properties, *structuralism* (Bird, 2007), and Humean-consistent accounts of properties, *quidditism* (Armstrong, 1997). The latter individuate properties in terms of something other than modal relations. See Wang (2016) and Demarest (2016) for introductions. For my own take, see Hildebrand (2016).

[61] For example, Cartwright (1999) and Williams (2019) place almost no constraints on the individuation of fundamental properties at all, as long as they are individuated in terms of some modal relations. As a result, some prefer different labels for their fundamental properties, such as 'powers' or 'capacities' or 'potencies'.

Dispositionalism (Vogt, 2022; Whittle, 2009). For our purposes, we don't need to worry too much about the details. But it's worth pointing out that Dispositionalism seems to have some theoretical flexibility that DTA does not.

To wrap up our discussion of Dispositionalism, let's consider Dispositionalist analyses of laws. According to the traditional view, laws are derived directly from the modal relations that individuate dispositional properties (Bird, 2007). For example, the above-mentioned Mass Axiom straightforwardly entails a lawlike regularity. Others hold that laws are generalizations in the best systematization of particular matters of fact, as in the BSA, except that particular matters of fact involve the instantiation of dispositions rather than Humean categorical properties (Demarest, 2017; Kimpton-Nye, 2017; Williams, 2019). Finally, some Dispositionalists hold that we can dispense with talk about laws entirely. Instead, we should, or at least can, reframe scientific discourse in terms of properties (Mumford, 2004). These approaches needn't differ with respect to *fundamental* entities or concepts. Their disagreement concerns the analysis of a concept that is *nonfundamental* by the lights of Dispositionalism. This is the same relationship that obtains between the Naïve Regularity Theory and the BSA.

Final remark: There is a relative of Dispositionalism that deserves to be mentioned before we move on: *Natural Kind Essentialism*. (Given more space, this view would have its own subsection.) Like Dispositionalism, it posits a type of modal structure internal to nature itself. However, it posits modal networks of *natural kinds* instead of *natural properties*. There are subtle but important differences between properties and kinds (Bird, 2018; Bird & Hawley, 2011), but here is a rough account of the distinction: A property, such as *being negatively charged*, is a single respect of similarity/resemblance, whereas a kind is "characterized by" clusters of properties, such as the cluster of properties (including *being negatively charged*) that categorize the kind *electron*. This can make it look like kinds are the result of binding dispositional properties together with a different species of necessity (Drewery, 2005; Keinanen & Tahko, 2019), but kinds are often taken to be more fundamental than the properties that characterize them. Proponents include Lowe (1989, 2006), Bigelow, Ellis, and Lierse (1992), Ellis (2001), Oderberg (2007), Tahko (2015), and Dumsday (2019).

4.3 General Taxonomy of Non-Humean Theories

Table 1 summarizes the Non-Humean theories we have examined in this section. Let's consider how they might fit into a broader classificatory scheme.[62]

Table 1 Overview of Non-Humean theories

	Fundamental Ontology	Conceptual Apparatus	Analysis of Laws
Humeanism	The mosaic of particular matters of fact	Concepts required to describe the mosaic	Reductive analysis along the lines of NRT or BSA
Divine Voluntarism	The mosaic of particular matters of fact plus God	Concepts required to describe the mosaic, plus the associated axiom(s) required to describe God and their relationship to the mosaic	Laws are divine decrees (vel sim)
Primitivism	The mosaic of particular matters of fact plus primitive laws	Concepts required to describe the mosaic, plus the axiom(s) required to describe primitive laws and their relationship to the mosaic	N/A, since laws are primitives
DTA	The mosaic of particular matters of fact plus universals plus nomic relations	Concepts required to describe the preceding entities, including axiom(s) for nomic relations	Laws are higher-order states of affairs consisting of nomic relations between universals

Table 1 (Continued.)

	Fundamental Ontology	Conceptual Apparatus	Analysis of Laws
Disposition-alism	The mosaic of particular *powerful* matters of fact (plus universals or tropes or ...)	Concepts required to describe the Dispositional-ist mosaic, including the axiom(s) for dispositions/powers	(i) laws derived from modal relations between properties OR (ii) as best systematization of Dispositionalist mosaic

If we're going to posit modal primitives, we have to put them somewhere. Non-Humeans have two general options. *Inflationary* theories add modal primitives that govern nature "from the outside." Examples include Divine Voluntarism, Primitivism, and DTA. In contrast, *revisionary* theories reinterpret the fundamental facts in nature as being modally laden, so that regularities arise "from within" nature.[63] Dispositionalism and Natural Kind Essentialism are examples of revisionary theories. To put this another way, inflationary theories reject the reductionist component of Humeanism, whereas revisionary theories reject the Humean characterization of nature as a Humean mosaic involving only non-modal properties.[64]

The inflationary/revisionary distinction is exhaustive but not exclusive. For example, one might accept that some fundamental facts in nature are irreducibly modal while also positing governing entities outside of the mosaic – perhaps because powers and governing laws are required to explain different sorts of regularities (Ioannidis, Livianos, & Psillos, 2021). And some versions of Dispositionalism and Natural Kind Essentialism appeal to God. Aquinas, for example, held that God created a world full of natural kind essences (Ott & Patton, 2018).[65]

---

[63] If you like, they "revise" Humeanism's account of the mosaic. I have chosen the label 'revisionary' for heuristical rather than historical reasons, since many Non-Humeans do not take Humeanism as their starting point.

[64] See Bhogal and Perry (2017, section 3) for a similar classification.

[65] For contemporary discussion of this sort of Divine Voluntarism, see Dumsday (2013, 145–146). Readers may wish to compare with Adams (2018), who argues that Divine Voluntarists should also accept Dispositionalism.

As we've seen, we can make finer divisions as well. On the inflationary side, natural necessity can be primitive or analyzable. If analyzable, it can involve intentionality (e.g., a god) or not. If not, it's natural to analyze laws of nature in terms of properties/universals, given the way properties feature in statements of laws. Thus, while Divine Voluntarism, Primitivism, and DTA aren't exhaustive of inflationary theories, they do cover a lot of logical space. Revisionary theories can be divided along similar lines. For example, Panpsychism about laws (Dolbeault, 2017) is a revisionary analogue of Divine Voluntarism, Lange's (2009) ontology of fundamental singular subjunctive facts looks like a revisionary analogue of Primitivism, and Dispositionalism is a revisionary analogue of DTA.[66] Finally, to reiterate a point made in Section 4.2.1 and Note 54, all of the above theories come in different varieties depending on the character of their modally robust primitives.

4.4 Conclusion

This concludes our overview of Non-Humean theories of laws. In Section 5, we'll consider conceptual objections to Non-Humeanism. And in Sections 6 and 7, we'll assess different versions of Non-Humeanism with the help of various criteria.

5 Conceptual Objections to Non-Humeanism

As we saw in the previous section, all versions of Non-Humeanism accept modally robust primitives. This is the source of some influential objections.

5.1 Modal Primitives are Unintelligible

One way to object to Non-Humeanism is simply to attack its conceptual machinery: to point to one of its fundamental concepts and say, "I don't understand that." Such objections usually rely on an implicit criterion, which I'll label for future reference:

Intelligibility Criterion: An adequate theory must not involve primitives we do not understand (Hildebrand, 2020b, 6).

David Hume famously argued that primitive necessary connections in nature are unintelligible (1748/2000, section 7).[67] If that's right, we're *incapable of*

---

[66] Barker and Smart (2012) nicely highlight the similarities between DTA and Dispositionalism.

[67] At least, Hume's argument is sometimes interpreted in the way that I'll present it. For ease of exposition, I'll speak as though this interpretation represents Hume's position, but I'm not committed to that view.

understanding any of the Non-Humean theories described in the preceding section.[68]

Hume's first premise provides a general criterion for the intelligibility of a concept:

Concept Empiricism: All intelligible concepts are either (i) copies of sense impressions or (ii) defined in terms of concepts that are copies of sense impressions.

Hume would say that I possess the concept of the color *gold* because I have been visually acquainted with the color and that I possess the concept of a *mountain* because I have been visually acquainted with mountains. Although I've never seen a gold mountain, I can combine the two concepts to form the concept of a *gold mountain*. The former two concepts are presented immediately in my experience; they are simply copies of impressions. The latter concept is not, but it is defined in terms of concepts that are.

Hume's second premise is that we have no sense impressions of necessity. (He focuses on *causal relations* in particular, but his argument is widely taken to apply to all modally robust primitive concepts.) For example, suppose you experience a rock breaking a window. Hume would say that you have visual and auditory impressions of shapes and colors and sounds but that there is simply no impression corresponding to the causal relation itself. All you see and hear are patterns among sense impressions. You might *infer* a causal connection from the patterns, but you don't *experience* it directly. Thus, the concept of causation cannot be a primitive concept corresponding to a simple impression; rather, it must be analyzed in terms of observed patterns.

Hume's conclusion is that primitive modality is unintelligible; we simply do not possess any primitive modal concepts. As you might suspect, Non-Humeans can object to either premise. Let's start with objections to the second premise.

Some philosophers believe that we do have sense impressions of necessity. Their strategy for responding to Hume's argument is simply to provide examples of the relevant impressions. We can divide them into two camps, depending on the type of impression they invoke. Hume accepts outward and inward sense impressions. Outward sensation concerns familiar senses such as sight and touch. Inward sensation concerns internal reflection, such as when

---

[68] What about theories that don't invoke *modal* primitives but instead opt for post-modal primitives such as essence or ground? As typically defined, such primitives entail necessary truths. If necessity is unintelligible, so too is any primitive that entails such necessity.

we examine our own thoughts and realize that there's something that it's like to think, to sense, to believe, etc.

Anscombe (1971), Fales (1990), and Armstrong (1983) propose examples involving outward sense impressions. For example, Anscombe suggests that we are directly acquainted with causal relations in everyday actions such as cutting butter with a knife. She claims that we literally experience the causal "force" or necessity as we push the knife. The tactile experience is modally rich.

Others, such as John Locke (1689/1975, book 2, chap. 21), propose examples involving inward sense impression (what Locke calls *reflection*). He suggests that internal reflection on your own will gives you the impression of active causal power. Consider your current desire to read this sentence. Now recall a happy memory. Now think about what it's like to desire, to remember, or to think. Locke would say that in performing these actions you have an inward sense impression of your own *power of will* to direct your attention as you see fit. Under favorable conditions, you are *capable* of getting what you want – in this case, of directing your mental attention to whatever you choose. Locke would say that if you don't use modal language here – using terms like 'power', 'ability', 'can', 'would' – you'll leave something out; you'll fail to accurately describe what it's like to reflect on the operation of your own mind.

Hume (1748/2000) is aware of these sorts of examples. He simply insists that we are acquainted merely with sequences of events that are (as far as we can tell) entirely loose and separate. We don't feel the causation when a knife cuts butter; we merely feel tactile pressure and see the butter dividing. We don't experience active causal powers of our will; we just experience one event (say, the desire) followed by another (say, the reflection). But make of this what you will. If, on sincere reflection, your own experiences seem modally rich, who is Hume to say otherwise? Maybe your experiences are richer than Hume's.

Let's turn to the second strategy. You might agree with Hume's interpretation of the cases above. But if you don't accept Concept Empiricism, Non-Humeanism might be intelligible anyway.

To begin, notice that Concept Empiricism is a bold, controversial philosophical thesis. What can be said in defense of it? Interestingly, Hume doesn't provide a direct argument. He merely offers it as part of a method of avoiding certain philosophical pitfalls – such as the pitfall of engaging in metaphysical speculation concerning questions we are unable to answer. Indeed, it is hard to see what an argument for Concept Empiricism could look like. There are often just two ways to defend big-picture methodological principles. First, we might find the principle appealing or intuitive. Second, the principle might be useful – say, for advancing certain theoretical goals. Suppose that metaphysicians have been sloppy in the way they define various concepts. Concept Empiricism *does* allow critiques of bad metaphysics, but it may not be *required* to critique bad metaphysics.

Let's consider some problems for Concept Empiricism. For starters, it has some unattractive consequences. Notably, it seems to require radical revision of many important ordinary concepts: notably, of causation, necessity, personal identity, God, and many others. Relatedly, it plays an important role in Hume's larger epistemological program, which is widely agreed to lead to skepticism about many important matters: induction, the external world, moral truths, and so on. In addition, Concept Empiricism seems to require a foundationalist story about the origin of our concepts, augmented by a strong version of the analytic/synthetic distinction, both of which are controversial.[69] For these reasons, Concept Empiricism is not widely accepted, nor are Hume's reasons for rejecting primitive modality.[70]

In addition, there is another positive case for thinking that modal concepts are intelligible. Suppose you reflect on your own concepts and find that the notion of metaphysical necessity seems perfectly clear and intelligible. Never mind how you acquired it. It seems perfectly intelligible to *you*. Perhaps you are acquainted with some formal tools for systematizing the concept and using it precisely – say, because you have a good grasp of modal logic. You can write down some axioms, prove various theorems, and construct models/interpretations of various systems. You know how to translate ordinary modal language into the formal language with the help of possible worlds semantics, and so on and so forth. Relatedly, suppose you could show that modal concepts are indispensable for articulating familiar everyday notions.[71] To mention just one example, certain everyday objects – such as chairs – might be defined by their functional role. But descriptions of functional role are often modal. For example, perhaps the role of a chair is to be *capable* of supporting weight. If that's right, ordinary discourse presupposes an understanding of modal concepts. If you can do any of these things, and the relevant modal concepts seem intelligible to you upon introspection, it's hard to see why you should accept Concept Empiricism, and thus it's hard to see why you should think that primitive necessities are unintelligible.

I've now provided a rough sketch of Hume's argument and some popular responses. Our discussion has been too brief to establish any firm conclusions,

---

[69] See Sellars (1956) and Quine (1951), respectively.

[70] For contemporary critical discussion of *Hume's dictum*, the principle (roughly stated) that there are no necessary connections between distinct existences, see J. Wilson (2010). See van Cleve (2018) for an overview of recent work sympathetic to Hume's dictum.

[71] For an extended defense of this sort of thesis, see Carroll (1994) on "nomic centrality."

but here's where I stand. Upon introspecting, I find primitive necessities intelligible. Moreover, with the development of modal logics and possible worlds semantics in particular, we have tools for precisely articulating Non-Humean theories – and in particular for modeling the way in which Non-Humean necessities constrain possibilities. Armed with our axioms for a given set of Non-Humean primitives, it's not difficult to demonstrate exactly how a carefully stated Non-Humean theory places restrictions on which sorts of models are admissible by the lights of the theory. These tools have been fruitful in many areas of metaphysics, and for these reasons it's hard to see why we should try to do without them entirely. This is not to say that there aren't interesting epistemological problems pertaining to primitive necessities. But philosophers can and should feel free to invoke such concepts in their theories.

5.2 The Inference Problem

Let's consider another popular objection to the conceptual apparatus of Non-Humeanism. We can illustrate with some simple questions posed to Divine Voluntarists and Primitivists, respectively: Why *must* God's will be done? Why *must* a primitive law bring about its associated regularity? Even if primitive necessities are intelligible, the specific way in which laws are supposed to necessitate their corresponding regularities may not be intelligible. To put a slightly different spin on the problem, Non-Humeanism seems to violate the following principle: If you posit a necessary connection between law and regularity, then you must *explain* it. You're not justified in making an inference from a law to its regularity unless you know *why* the regularity has to follow from the law. This is known as *the inference problem* (see Lewis, 1983, 366; van Fraassen, 1989, 38–39, 96–102).

Treated as an objection to Non-Humeanism, the inference problem consists of two main steps. First, articulate a criterion for a theory of laws:

Inference Criterion: A theory must include an account of the connection between laws (or the modal entities it posits) and regularities.

Second, argue that the theory cannot satisfy the criterion. As it turns out, however, this is surprisingly difficult to do.

Consider the question "Why *must* God's will be done?" Here is a natural answer from Divine Voluntarists: "Because it's built right into the concept of God! After all, we *defined* God as a being with that power." Given the Omnipotence Axiom from Section 4.2.1, this answer is trivial. The interesting question is whether the axiom itself is intelligible. But it seems to be intelligible insofar as modality is intelligible. Exactly the same is true for Primitivism: If its axiom for primitive laws is intelligible, the question "Why *must* a primitive law bring about its associated regularity?" has a trivial answer. Arguably it is similar for *all* Non-Humean theories. *If* you grant Non-Humeans their primitives – that is, if you let them axiomatize their primitives as we did in Section 4 – then the inference problem is trivially easy to solve.

Schaffer (2016) calls these *axiomatic solutions* to the inference problem.[72] The basic idea is this. Whenever we introduce a new primitive, we can – indeed, we must – outfit the primitive with axioms specifying the theoretical role(s) of the primitive and its relation(s) to other primitives in our metaphysics. Thus, provided that God is intelligible, Divine Voluntarism automatically satisfies the Inference Criterion. So too do the other Non-Humean theories we have considered. Critics can object to the intelligibility of the modality involved (or to other concepts required to state the axioms in question) but that is to invoke the Intelligibility Criterion rather than the Inference Criterion.

Thus, proponents of the inference problem encounter a dilemma: If they grant Non-Humeans their conceptual machinery, the inference problem admits of an utterly trivial solution (the axiomatic solution); but if they don't grant the conceptual machinery, the objection collapses into the the original unintelligibility objection discussed in Section 5.1.

Here's another explanation of this point. The Inference Criterion says that a theory of laws must "include an account" of the connection between laws and regularities. There are different ways to account for an element of a metaphysical theory. You can analyze an element in terms of other elements. Or you can treat an element as primitive, in which case you need to say something about how we're to understand the primitive, its theoretical role, etc. Interestingly, this methodological point is made by David Lewis (1983) in the very same paper in which he raises a version of the inference problem.[73] He argues that proponents of natural properties do *not* need to analyze naturalness. They can accept it as primitive.

> Not every *account* is an *analysis*! A system that takes certain Moorean facts as primitive, as unanalysed, cannot be accused of failing to make a place for them. It neither shirks the compulsory question nor answers it by denial. It does give an account. (Lewis, 1983, 352, original emphasis)

At the end of the day, everyone needs some primitives. For this reason, I believe that the inference problem collapses into something else. Perhaps it collapses

---

[72] See Coates (in press) for a critical response.

[73] For this reason, I suspect that Lewis is actually concerned with the older Intelligibility Criterion rather than the Inference Criterion. His desire to avoid unanalyzable modality is an enduring theme in his work. See especially Lewis (1986a).

into the older problem concerning the intelligibility of modal concepts (I think this is closest to the spirit of the problem as usually raised). Perhaps it collapses into a problem of ontological economy. Or perhaps it collapses into a problem concerning that which gets explained: Humeans can explain the necessary connection between law and regularity as a simple consequence of the fact that laws reduce to regularities; in contrast, Non-Humeans who employ an axiomatic solution must simply stipulate the connection.

5.3 One Last Conceptual Objection

I have intentionally overlooked a different interpretation of the inference problem. This is because I prefer to treat it as a different conceptual objection. Suppose you think that human persons are essentially embodied but that God is essentially immaterial. You might not understand the Omnipotence Axiom, because the concept of a personal God is too dissimilar to your concept of a human person. Or suppose that, like Armstrong (1997), you claim that all universals are *categorical*, which is to say that they lack any intrinsic modal character. Or suppose that, like Tooley (1977), you claim that an analysis of laws must proceed in entirely non-nomic terms, which Tooley interprets as avoiding primitive modality. In either case, you may have a hard time understanding how DTA's nomic relations could be given the *modal* characterization I offered in the Nomic Necessitation Axiom.[74] As these cases suggest, the mere intelligibility of modal concepts does not mean that any theory employing modal concepts will be intelligible. Theories must be internally consistent! There are many ways to run afoul of that requirement, regardless of whether one employs primitive modal concepts.

In some cases, there is an easy fix. Armstrong could maintain that most universals are categorical, while recognizing that nomic relations are special. Tooley could emphasize that there are benefits to analyzing laws in terms of other primitives, while embracing the fact that at least one such primitive must have irreducible modal character. I suspect that much of the confusion surrounding the inference problem arises precisely because Armstrong and Tooley make an effort to downplay the modal primitives involved in their theory of laws. This leads to the appearance of internal inconsistency.

I'll mention one other example of a problem in this vicinity. There is a well-known objection that certain forms of Dispositionalism lead to a metaphysical circularity or regress. We have focused on Dispositionalism as a theory of laws, but it is also a theory of properties. Some philosophers endorse the strong claim

---

[74] See Bird (2005) and Coates (2021) for discussion of this objection to DTA.

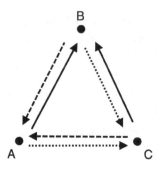

Figure 2 A symmetrical structure of dispositions

that fundamental dispositional properties are individuated *solely* by their modal relations to other properties. Let's call this view *Strong Dispositionalism*. Consider a world that exhibits the following regularities among three fundamental properties: For all properties X, Y, and Z, whenever two objects with distinct properties X and Y encounter one another each of them loses its original property and acquires distinct property Z. We can posit a structure of fundamental dispositions of the sort illustrated in Figure 2. The hatching indicates relations of mutual manifestation. Thus, for example, the pair of solid lines from A to B and from C to B represents the fact that A and C mutually manifest B. This graph exhibits perfect symmetry. As a result, its nodes cannot be distinguished in purely relational terms. This conflicts with Strong Dispositionalism's claim that properties are individuated solely by their relations to other properties. There are different ways to try to develop this apparent conflict into a more careful objection to Strong Dispositionalism, but I'll simply mention two ways to avoid it.[75] One option is to bite the bullet: grant that Strong Dispositionalism is incompatible with symmetrical structures of properties but argue that Strong Dispositionalism might turn out to be the best theory of laws for worlds with asymmetric structures. Another option is to reject Strong Dispositionalism in favor of a weaker version of Dispositionalism. Dispositionalists could expand the individuation conditions for properties so that they include something more than mere modal relations.[76]

5.4 Conclusion

Although conceptual objections to Non-Humeanism have been influential, they are far from decisive. Nonetheless, studying them is valuable, because they at

---

[75] See Bird (2007) for an overview of and responses to regress objections to Dispositionalism.

[76] See, for example, Heil (2003), Jacobs (2011), Williams (2019), Tugby (2021), Coates (2020), and Kimpton-Nye (2021).

least reinforce an important lesson: We must choose our primitives wisely, and we must take care to integrate them into our larger theories.

6 Further Problems for Non-Humean Theories

In Section 2, we considered extensional objections to Humeanism. In this section, we'll consider related objections to Non-Humean theories. Some seem to classify too many statements as laws, and others too few.

6.1 Problems for Property-Based Theories of Laws

To begin, we'll consider some problem cases for DTA and Dispositionalism. These problem cases share a common structure, in that they suggest the Non-Humean theories fail to satisfy the following extensional criterion:

Scientific Criterion: A theory of laws should classify the laws of our best scientific theories (in this world and in other possible worlds) as laws.

6.1.1 Functional Laws

Armstrong argues that proponents of the Naïve Regularity Theory struggle to accommodate *functional* laws. This is a problem, because a typical statement of law in a modern scientific theory is not expressible in the language of first-order logic; it is a mathematical function relating quantities of various properties.

Some Non-Humean theories seem to have no trouble accommodating functional laws (or, more broadly, the Scientific Criterion). Consider Primitivism. In Section 4.2.2, we axiomatized the primitive law operator so that its being a law that p entails p. Because primitive laws don't have any internal metaphysical structure, there aren't any restrictions on the contents of sentence p. Any sentence can be plugged in! Thus, Primitivists can posit a primitive law corresponding to any statement of law found in any possible scientific theory. Divine Voluntarism appears to be similar in this respect. Any law a scientist could posit seems to describe a regularity that God could decree. On the surface, these views don't place major restrictions on the contents of statements of laws.

However, DTA and Dispositionalism may not satisfy the Scientific Criterion as easily. It's easy to posit nomic relations and dispositions that explain toy regularities such as that *all Fs are Gs* and *all Ds become M under conditions C*. However, it's not obvious how to extend these accounts to cover the functional laws distinctive of modern science. The mathematical function must be written into the properties and relations of the theory, and this gives rise to some difficulties.[77]

One difficulty is that some statements of laws do not involve fundamental properties. To illustrate, let's consider an example from Hicks and Schaffer (2017).[78] Suppose our world is Newtonian. Acceleration is defined as the second derivative of position. Thus, the following two equations are mathematically equivalent:

$$F = ma \tag{6.1}$$

$$F = m\frac{d^2x}{dt^2} \tag{6.2}$$

This raises a question. Which properties does the law actually relate? To which universal (or universals) does the 'a' in '$F = ma$' correspond? Acceleration seems more relevant than position, because Newton's second law exhibits various symmetries: for example, acceleration is invariant under universal positional transformations. If the locations of everything were shifted uniformly, there would be no changes in acceleration but there would be changes in absolute position. Thus, acceleration, rather than position, seems to be the property that actually matters. But if acceleration is a *derived* quantity, presumably it can't be a *fundamental* universal. At the very least, proponents of property-based theories owe us an account of how to treat functional laws involving derived quantities.[79]

Another difficulty is that incorporating functional laws into the analysis of nomic relations (or of individuation conditions for dispositions or natural kinds) seems to undermine the importance of properties in the first place. To illustrate, let's take a closer look at Tooley's account of nomic relations. Recall that our Nomic Necessitation Axiom mapped the relation N to a regularity by way of a function. Namely, it is necessary that whenever N binds two universals all instances of the first are instances of the second. Tooley's general account of nomic relations specifies that all nomic relations are defined in terms of a "construction function" that maps the higher-order relation (N^*) and the properties it relates ($P_1, \ldots P_n$) to some regularity among their instances. Thus, any axiom for a nomic relation N^* must stipulate that $N^*(P_1, \ldots P_n)$ gives rise to some regularity among instances of $P_1, \ldots P_n$. But *which* regularity? Well, it could be

---

[77] For general objections of this sort, see Armstrong (1983, chap. 7), Vetter (2009, 2012), and Collins (2009).

[78] For related discussion, see M. Wilson (1987) and Chen and Goldstein (2022).

[79] I offer a response to Hicks and Schaffer (2017) in Hildebrand (2019b). Proponents of DTA can insist that the law itself is more complex than $F = ma$ suggests, because it involves relations of relative position rather than acceleration, though this solution is not without its difficulties.

anything. For example, we can let N^S be the nomic relation that underlies the Schrödinger equation, and $P_1, \ldots P_n$ the properties involved in that equation. Then the construction function for relation N^S essentially *just is* the Schrödinger equation. This seems like a reasonable way to account for functional laws, but it raises a question: Why should we bother with the metaphysics of universals instead of positing primitive laws? If we need to write the scientific statement of law into the nomic relation, it's not clear that there's any work for the universals to do.

6.1.2 Conservation Laws

Dispositionalists are thought to have a hard time accommodating conservation laws. Alexander Bird nicely summarizes the difficulty they pose:

> Conservation and symmetry laws tell us that interactions are constrained by the requirement of preserving, e.g., mass-energy or momentum. But that constraint does not appear to be the manifesting of a disposition. (Bird, 2007, 211)[80]

To elaborate slightly, consider the conservation law for mass-energy. It says that mass-energy of a closed system remains the same through all interactions within the system. We might suggest that all systems have a disposition to preserve mass-energy in the absence of external interferences, but that seems to raise more questions than answers. For one, a *system* is a macro-phenomenon, and it can seem strange that such a thing would possess a fundamental dispositional property. For another, the disposition in question refers to *absences*. But what are they? It might be tempting to posit a disposition whose stimulus condition is the presence of a *noninterference property*. However, most proponents of natural properties treat negative properties like gruesome properties: Their instances needn't have anything in common, so they aren't natural.[81] For these reasons, positing dispositions of systems is somewhat unattractive.

In response, some Dispositionalists posit a new sort of natural necessity. For example, Bigelow et al. (1992) suggest that there are *kinds of worlds* and that conservation laws flow from the essences of such kinds. Dispositionalists could augment their view with kind essences of this sort. They might also treat conservation laws as primitive laws, or DTA laws, etc. However, in addition to requiring new varieties of primitive necessity – relative to Dispositionalism in a more standard form – these solutions seem ad hoc (Bird, 2007, 213).

A different option is to give conservation laws special treatment. This treatment will depend on one's underlying theory of laws. Symmetry principles

---

[80] See also Schurz (2011) and French (2014).
[81] See Armstrong (1989b, 82–84), Armstrong (1997, 27), and Rodriguez-Pereyra (2002, 51).

describe invariances in our laws under different sorts of transformations. They are meta-laws of a sort. As Bird points out, Humeans can treat symmetry principles as regularities about regularities;[82] DTA can treat them as third-order relations that constrain nomic relations. In both cases, the views seem to be imposing constraints on lawhood. However, since Dispositionalists think that properties are individuated by modal relations, the laws seem to be metaphysically necessary and therefore not in need of further external constraints. Thus, Bird suggests that Dispositionalists might hold that "symmetry principles and conservation laws will be eliminated as being features of our form of representation rather than features of the world requiring to be accommodated within our metaphysics" (Bird, 2007, 214).

6.1.3 Special Science Laws

Laws in the special sciences have a different character than laws in fundamental physics. In particular, the former admit of exceptions, apply in fewer circumstances, and generally seem less stable. As noted in Section 2.8, there are three main responses to problems posed by such laws. First, we could say that special science "laws" aren't really laws. That seems to place philosophical constraints on scientific practice, which some find undesirable. Second, we could provide a reduction of special science laws to fundamental laws of physics. This may seem possible in principle, but it is no small task. Third, we could provide an account of special science laws that does not reduce them to physical laws. The question is, how should such an account proceed if one accepts Non-Humeanism?

Some Non-Humeans may have difficulty answering this question.[83] For example, Cohen and Callender (2009) argue that Lewis's Naturalness Constraint makes his version of the BSA ill-suited to analyze laws in the special sciences, for the simple reason that some properties referenced in special science theories are *not* perfectly natural. If that's right, Non-Humean theories committed to a naturalness constraint – these include DTA and Bird's version of Dispositionalism – would have similar difficulties. Thus, they would be forced either to deny that there are special science laws or to show how to reduce them to physical laws. Those who wish to accept special science laws at face value would need to seek a different Non-Humean theory. I'll briefly sketch two possible examples.

---

[82] For recent discussions, see Lange (2009), Hicks (2019), and Friend (in press).

[83] I suspect that Primitivists and Divine Voluntarists may also, given the unique modal character of special science laws, but I'll focus on property-based theories here.

As we saw in Section 4.2.4, some Dispositionalists accept a Non-Humean description of the mosaic in which fundamental properties are powers or dispositions and analyze laws as generalizations in the best systematization of their Non-Humean mosaic. We can take this a step further by interpreting the notion of a best system pragmatically, just like Pragmatic Humeans.[84] This approach suggests a promising analysis of special science laws in part because, as with Pragmatic Humeanism, the analysis of law is somewhat divorced from events at the fundamental level. It allows us to pick and choose domains of facts to systematize.

The second approach is a bit different. At the beginning of this subsection, I said that special science laws have a different character than fundamental physical laws. However, it may be that fundamental laws are just as messy as special science laws: all laws are subject to provisos or *ceteris paribus* conditions; all laws are sensitive to background conditions; no laws hold with strict necessity; and so on.[85] For example, Cartwright (1999) holds that properties in nature are *capacities* to behave – a species of power or disposition. Capacities can be instantiated at different levels, but not all macro-level capacities reduce to micro-level capacities. In general, capacities at one level needn't have priority over capacities at another. In worlds like this, simple universal generalizations cannot be statements of laws, because they will not be true. However, that does not mean that nature is devoid of patterns. Capacities have modal character, and they will reliably generate patterns *under the right conditions*.[86] Statements of law, then, are generalizations that hold under carefully specified background conditions as a result of worldly capacities. This holds for physical laws and special science laws alike.

In sum, Non-Humeans have options for dealing with the problem posed by special science laws. Depending on what one wishes to say about special science laws, the practice of science may give us reason to prefer some theories over others.

6.1.4 Recap

I have provided brief overviews of the problems posed by functional laws, conservation laws, and special science laws for certain Non-Humean theories. My goal has been merely to illuminate the structure of these problems and some of their potential solutions. I don't claim to offer any assessment of these or any

---

[84] For a defense of this sort of view, see Kimpton-Nye (2021).

[85] See Cartwright (1999) and Kistler (2006) for defenses of this position.

[86] Cartwright's detailed proposal relies on the notion of a *nomological machine*, which is a sort of mechanism defined in terms of the capacities of things operating within a given stable framework (such as a laboratory experiment, or certain kind regions of nature).

of the other myriad problems of this form, except to note that the type of solutions involved differ from theory to theory, in such a way that some solutions might incur serious costs. In addition to the laws discussed in this section, it has been argued that property-based varieties of Non-Humeanism struggle to accommodate idealized laws (Tan, 2020), regularities that things are disposed to retain their dispositions over time in the absence of interferences (Tugby, 2017), and putatively lawlike boundary conditions such as the Past Hypothesis according to which the universe began in a low entropy state (Chen, in press).[87] Nevertheless, here is a general lesson.

Non-Humean theories introduce metaphysical structure into their analyses of laws to varying degrees. The type and amount of structure introduced have some important implications. A theory with too much structure, or the wrong kind of structure, may have difficulty accommodating the Scientific Criterion. Suppose some Non-Humean theory can't make sense of functional laws, conservation laws, or symmetrical structures of regularities (see Section 5.3). If we were wedded to that theory, we would have to place constraints on scientific theorizing: namely our final scientific theory must avoid functional laws, conservation laws, symmetrical sets of laws/properties, etc. Metaphysicians should be wary of placing such constraints on scientific theorizing.[88]

6.2 Problems for Divine Voluntarism and Primitivism

As I suggested in Section 6.1, Divine Voluntarism and Primitivism are flexible theories. They seem to accommodate the Scientific Criterion. However, that does not imply that they are extensionally adequate. They might allow for too many laws.

To begin, let's consider a problem for Divine Voluntarism. It might struggle to distinguish between lawlike and accidental regularities because it allows for different sorts of divine decrees. We can imagine a God saying:

(1) Let massive objects obey Newton's laws.
(2) Let this particular jug of water be wine.
(3) Let nature be thus and so, down to every last detail.

The first looks like a lawlike decree. The second looks like a miracle – an exception to the laws rather than a law itself. The third decree aligns with certain religious doctrines concerning God's sovereignty: If every fact is ultimately

---

[87] See Adlam (2022) for further examples of laws that are not amenable to a property-based analysis.

[88] See Hildebrand (2020a) for a more careful discussion of this problem.

willed by God, then God stands in the same modal relationship to all facts. Their necessity is the same! This is reminiscent of the problem with Lewis's predicate F.[89] Thus, Divine Voluntarists must distinguish between decrees that are lawlike and those that aren't. There are options, but they incur some costs.

First, Divine Voluntarists might stipulate that laws correspond only to a proper subset of divine decrees, namely, those that are axioms in the best systematization of nature. Decree (2) isn't part of the best system, so it's not a law. Nor is (3), at least when we restrict our system to eligible languages involving only perfectly natural predicates. This approach seems promising, but it concedes a lot to Humeans. God plays a relatively small role in this account of laws. Perhaps God is the source of necessity in nature, but that necessity doesn't suffice for lawhood. The distinction between laws and accidents relies on something else entirely.

Second, Divine Voluntarists could say more about *how* God creates a world full of regularities. For example, perhaps God creates a world governed by primitive laws, or nomic relations between universals, or fundamental dispositions, etc. The laws, then, will correspond to divine decrees concerning the creation of these entities. This concedes a lot to other versions of Non-Humeanism. With these entities in the picture, we might have no use for God.

Similar problems can arise for Primitivism, albeit in a slightly different way. Primitivists stipulate that lawhood is primitive, but they still need to say something about *which* sorts of facts are eligible to be considered laws. Suppose we recast (1), (2), and (3) as declarative sentences. Could those sentences simply be statements of law? In principle, I don't see why not. As mentioned, our axiom for primitive laws places no restrictions on the contents of sentences to which the law operator can attach. According to our version of Primitivism, it *could* be a law that this glass of water turns to wine, or that things are thus and so down to every last detail. But these do not seem like statements of laws even if they are necessary in the relevant sense. Thus, primitivists need to say more about what makes primitive necessities lawlike. We'll briefly examine two approaches.

Carroll suggests that statements of laws are true, general or universal, and contingent (1994, 21–22). Suppose we interpret this suggestion as imposing

---

[89] This concern overlaps with a traditional worry about the *Principle of Sufficient Reason*, according to which all facts have a sufficient explanation. We seem to have lost the commonsense distinction between necessity and contingency. But see Dasgupta (2016) for an argument that this consequence is not as problematic as it might appear.

constraints on sentences eligible to be bound by the 'it is a law that' operator. Unfortunately, these restrictions don't seem to correspond to our notion of law. As will be familiar from our discussion of the Naïve Regularity Theory, many accidental regularities are true, universal, and contingent. And some putatively lawlike regularities lack such features. As a result, our ordinary concept of law doesn't align with the constraints inspired by Carroll's suggestion.

According to Maudlin, laws describe how states of a system evolve over time; they are "fundamental laws of temporal evolution" (2007, 10–15). This, too, constrains the sentences eligible to be laws, but perhaps by too much. Here is a nice example from Chen and Goldstein (2022, 43–44) of a law in an atemporal world. The Mandelbrot set is produced by a simple rule: A complex number is a member of this set if and only if the function $f_c(z) = z^2 + c$ does not diverge when iterated starting from $z = 0$. Don't worry if you don't understand the function. What matters for our purposes is just that (i) the function is very simple and (ii) when the members of this set are mapped to the complex plane, the result is a striking fractal pattern.[90] Now consider a timeless two-dimensional world in which the distribution of matter matches the fractal pattern of the Mandelbrot set. We may regard the distribution of matter as resulting from a simple atemporal law. Thus, Maudlin's constraints seem a bit too restrictive to capture our concept of law.[91]

Once again, our discussion has been brief. I don't claim that all versions of Divine Voluntarism and Primitivism are extensionally inadequate. However, there is a danger that such accounts may not be as illuminating as we'd like. It's one thing to say that laws involve a primitive sort of necessity; it's another thing to show how primitive necessity allows us to distinguish between laws and accidents.

6.3 Conclusion

Extensional adequacy is hard to achieve. Property-based theories struggle to account for certain statements of laws. This is due to the robust metaphysical structure of their accounts. In their most general forms, Primitivism and Divine Voluntarism struggle to account for the fact that certain statements are not and could not be statements of laws. This is due to the comparative lack of structure. Is there a middle ground? I don't know. A more careful examination of these issues is required.

---

[90] I suggest finding a .gif or video file that "zooms in" on the Mandelbrot set.
[91] See Adlam (2022) for similar criticism.

7 The Explanatory Argument for Non-Humeanism

7.1 Introduction

In this section, we'll examine an argument that Non-Humeanism provides the best explanation of observed regularities. Owing to space constraints, we won't carefully examine other intensional criteria – notably, concerning counterfactuals and induction. However, to a large extent intensional criteria go hand in hand. If there are lawlike regularities of a sort that can't be explained by Non-Humean laws, it will be hard for Non-Humeans to claim that their laws support counterfactuals or inductive inferences concerning those regularities either. If we have to focus on a single intensional criterion, it is appropriate to focus on questions of explanatory power.

I should also point out that *Humeans* have a great interest in assessing explanatory credentials, because that is crucial for assessing a major motivation for their view: its economy. Typically, considerations of economy come into play only *when all else is equal*. If Non-Humeanism has explanatory advantages, it won't be the case that all else is equal.

7.2 A Toy Example

Before stating the explanatory argument for Non-Humeanism, let's consider a toy example. This will help to clarify its form and identify some important assumptions.

Dice: I have a 100-sided die. I roll it ten times in a row, and each time I roll a 100. Now consider these hypotheses:

Fair (*F*): The die is fair.

Cheating (*C*): I manipulated the die somehow.

Presumably you prefer *C* to *F*. The observed sequence *S* is much more likely if I'm cheating than if I'm playing fairly. Although (surely!) it might seem implausible that someone of my character would cheat, it's more plausible than that *S* would occur by chance ($1 * 10^{-20}$, or one in one hundred quintillion). As a result, *C* is a better explanation than *S*.

We can make this argument more precise by interpreting it in a probabilistic form. Here is an equation known as the odds form of Bayes's theorem:

$$\frac{P(H_1|O)}{P(H_2|O)} = \frac{P(O|H_1)P(H_1)}{P(O|H_2)P(H_2)} \tag{7.1}$$

We'll unpack this from right to left. The terms $P(H_1)$ and $P(H_2)$ are *prior probabilities*. They describe how probable each hypothesis is prior to observation O. The terms $P(O|H_1)$ and $P(O|H_2)$ are *likelihoods*. These conditional probabilities describe how probable the observation O is given each hypothesis H. Finally, the terms on the left, $P(H_1|O)$ and $P(H_2|O)$, are *posterior probabilities*. These conditional probabilities describe how probable a hypothesis H is given an observation O. If you like, you can think of posterior probabilities as specifying the degree of confidence you (ought to) have in each hypothesis *after* observing O. On an intuitive level, Bayes's theorem says that the best explanation among our hypotheses is the one with the best balance of two virtues: prior (the initial plausibility of the hypothesis) and likelihood (the ability of a hypothesis to make sense of an observation).

Let's apply this to our case **Dice**, using Bayes's theorem to structure our argument.

$$\frac{P(C|S)}{P(F|S)} = \frac{P(S|C)P(C)}{P(S|F)P(F)} \tag{7.2}$$

Presumably $P(F)$ is greater than $P(C)$, because fair play is more common than competent cheating. However, it seems that $P(S|C)$ is *much* greater than $P(S|F)$. $P(S|F)$ is just $1 * 10^{-20}$, but rolling a bunch of 100s seems like the sort of thing your cheating philosophy professor might do. Thus, the ratio $\frac{P(S|C)}{P(S|F)}$ is *much* greater than the ratio $\frac{P(F)}{P(C)}$. This entails that $P(C|S) > P(F|S)$, so the cheating hypothesis is the better explanation of my sequence of rolls.

In case it's helpful, we can visualize these probabilities with the help of Figure 3, in which probabilities correspond to region size. The Cheating box (light gray, regions 1 & 2) is smaller than the Fair box (dark gray, regions 3 & 4). Thus, $P(C) < P(F)$. The Observed sequence box (lined, regions 2 & 4) overlaps the Cheating and Fair boxes. However, there is greater overlap with Cheating than with Fair (region 2 > region 4). With that in place, the diagram provides a clear way to visualize the ratio $P(F|S) : P(C|S)$. It is simply the ratio *region 2 :*

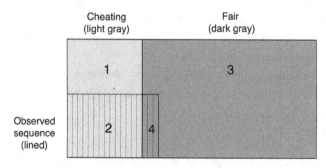

Figure 3 Probabilities in our game of dice

region 4. Upon learning that you're somewhere in the lined box, you're more likely to be in the light box than the dark box.

Before moving on, I'd like to make some clarifications about the probabilities involved in this example.[92] They're *epistemic probabilities*. They describe the degree of support you have for accepting the relevant propositions, given your total evidence. Thus, in saying that $P(C) < P(F)$, I'm saying that before observing S you ought to be more confident in F than in C. In saying that $P(S|C) \gg P(S|F)$, I'm saying that you ought to be much more confident that S would occur if C were the case than if F were the case.[93] I'm not saying that these probabilities describe your actual first-person subjective degrees of confidence (these are called *credences*), though I hope they do! I'm not saying that all of these probabilities describe *physical probabilities / objective chances* in the natural world. For example, the probability that a die comes up 100 is, or is determined by, physical features of the die itself. However, in the present example you're trying to figure out whether I cheated, given some evidence. That's an epistemological project rather than a metaphysical one, even though various hypotheses about the nature of the die are relevant to what you ought to believe.

A disclaimer: There are substantive epistemological assumptions underlying the arguments discussed in this section. For example, I'm assuming that we can assign prior probabilities, but this is a substantive assumption in its own right, especially when they're taken to be objective.[94] In addition, there are worries about the assignment of probabilities to unbounded sample spaces, which are difficult to normalize.[95] There are also general worries about the assignment

---

[92] For introductions to interpretations of probability, see Mellor (2005) and Hàjek (2019).

[93] I'm speaking somewhat loosely here, because statements of conditional probability are not probabilities of conditionals.

[94] Some philosophers don't think that there are any objective constraints on epistemic probabilities – i.e., on the credences one ought to have – beyond the theorems of the probability calculus. For example, some will say that there are no constraints whatsoever on the assignment of prior probabilities. Anything goes, as long as the probabilities (of non-tautologies) are between 0 and 1. (Weisberg (2019) provides an accessible introduction to what is known as *the problem of the priors*. This is closely related to the old empiricist objection that rational intuition is mysterious, applied to probabilistic contexts. As such, it is also related to van Fraassen's (1989, chap. 6) well-known objections to inference to the best explanation. See Huemer (2017) for an argument that we need a method of assigning objective priors to avoid skepticism.) If that's your view, the argument above would show that it's rational to believe that I'm cheating *if* you agree with my assignment of priors – a less interesting conclusion to be sure but still one that has epistemological character. In the next section, I'll argue that such conclusions remain interesting for the metaphysics of laws.

[95] See Manson (2009) for an accessible introduction and relevant citations.

of probabilities to metaphysical hypotheses.[96] I don't have the space to discuss all of these assumptions in this section, let alone to defend them. However, for the purposes of introducing the explanatory argument for Non-Humeanism and identifying some crucial challenges, we can set these aside.

7.3 The Explanatory Argument

The explanatory argument for Non-Humeanism (or some version thereof) has the same basic form as the argument we just considered: Just as the cheating hypothesis is better than the fair hypothesis in light of sequence S, so Non-Humeanism (or some version of it) is supposedly better than Humeanism in light of observed regularities in nature.[97] The two cases feel analogous. Regularities in nature seem to call out for an explanation, just like my sequence of 100s. Positing a cheater involves positing something outside the sequence of rolls; likewise, positing a God or primitive laws or relations between universals involves positing something outside of nature.[98] And since Humeanism ultimately takes the distribution of events as a brute fact – while treating all other distributions of events as being on a par with the actual one – it feels akin to explaining the distribution by an appeal to mere chance.

As above, we can use the odds form of Bayes's theorem to structure a more precise version of the argument.

$$\frac{P(N|R)}{P(H|R)} = \frac{P(R|N)P(N)}{P(R|H)P(H)} \tag{7.3}$$

We'll use N for Non-Humeanism, H for Humeanism, and R for the proposition that nature contains regularities. To clarify, R doesn't say that nature contains some specific set of regularities – we don't yet know which set that is! Rather, it just says that nature contains *some* set or other.

Let's begin with the priors. Humeanism and Non-Humeanism are broad metaphysical hypotheses. In fact, they're mutually exclusive and jointly exhaustive.[99] The sum of their probabilities is 1, so $P(N \vee H) = 1$. But how should we distribute this probability among these hypotheses? I won't try to arrive at a precise number, but here are some general reasons to assign them somewhat

---

[96] Filomeno (2019) provides a general defense of the claim that we can assign probabilities in the context of explanatory arguments against Humeanism.

[97] For defenses of the argument in various forms, see Fales (1990), Bird (2007, 86–90), Foster (2004), Tooley (2011), Hildebrand (2013), Filomeno (2019), and Hildebrand and Metcalf (2022).

[98] The hypothesis *that the die is weighted* is analogous to revisionary versions of Non-Humeanism, whereas the hypothesis that I'm a skilled roller of dice is analogous to inflationary versions of Non-Humeanism.

[99] At least, they're exhaustive if we treat Humeanism as the bare bones hypothesis that there is no primitive necessity.

similar values – say, within an order of magnitude of one another.[100] To begin, both are very general metaphysical hypotheses. The notion of generality here can be a little hard to pin down, so here's an example of a not-at-all general hypothesis:

Unicorns! (U): Nature consists of exactly four unicorns eternally galloping in a circle of radius 100 m on a Euclidean plane.

$P(U \lor \neg U) = 1$, but $P(\neg U) \gg P(U)$. This is because U is an extremely narrow, highly specific hypothesis. It is logically incompatible with anything that *we* could possibly observe (unless you and I could be unicorns). In contrast, Humeanism and Non-Humeanism exhibit a kind of symmetry: both are extremely general; neither logically conflicts with any possible observation; and both are compatible with a broad range of metaphysical hypotheses about other philosophical issues. Recall the distinction between scientific and philosophical questions about laws from Section 1. Humeanism and Non-Humeanism in their general forms are sufficiently general and abstract that neither conflicts with any possible account of the contents of statements of scientific laws. Granted, Non-Humeanism is less parsimonious than Humeanism, and that may count for something. But if we suppose that Non-Humeanism is intelligible – and let's be honest, those who are convinced that it's unintelligible probably stopped reading at the end of Section 5 – then arguably these differences don't count for much. Thus, I think the values of $P(H)$ and $P(N)$ are pretty similar. I'll grant that $P(H) > P(N)$ for the sake of argument, but I deny that $P(H) \gg P(N)$.

Let's turn to the likelihoods, beginning with $P(R|H)$. Arguably such probabilities can be determined simply by looking at the contents of theories. Humeanism has two crucial features. First, Humeanism accepts a recombination principle according to which there are no constraints on distributions of events in spacetime; every logically consistent distribution is possible. As a result, the set of epistemically possible Humean worlds is large and diverse; the vast majority of its worlds don't include widespread regularities. Second, Humeanism treats the actuality of our world – the fact that we have this distribution of events as opposed to another – as a brute, primitive fact. Nothing about Humeanism suggests that we can assign a higher prior probability to some possible worlds than others; in fact, since one Humean mosaic is just as good as the next, Humeanism seems to require a uniform probability distribution in which each Humean world has the same probability. In sum, regularities occur only in a tiny proportion of epistemically possible Humean possible worlds, but we

---

[100] For more detail, see Draper (2017) and Hildebrand and Metcalf (2022, section 5).

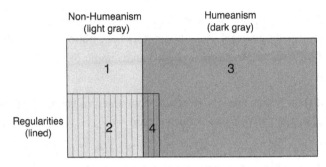

Figure 4 Probabilities in the explanatory argument

have no good reason to assign the regular Humean worlds more probability than the irregular Humean worlds. Thus, $P(R|H)$ is extremely low.[101]

The situation for Non-Humeanism appears different: We should assign $P(R|N)$ a much higher value than we assigned to $P(R|H)$. Non-Humeanism rejects the Humean recombination principle. The primitive necessities distinctive of Non-Humean theories constrain distributions of events. If God decrees that nature obey Newton's laws, it must, and similarly for other versions of Non-Humeanism. As a result, the set of epistemically possible Non-Humean possible worlds does not appear as diverse as the set of Humean possible worlds.[102] Indeed, one might think that regularities are practically *inevitable* given Non-Humeanism. We don't need such a strong claim though. Since $P(R|H)$ is extremely low, it doesn't take much for $P(R|N)$ to be significantly greater.

Let's put these premises together. The difference between the priors isn't that great: $P(H) > P(N)$. But the difference between the likelihoods is enormous: $P(R|N) \gg P(R|H)$. By Bayes's theorem, $P(N|R) > P(H|R)$. Thus, Non-Humeanism is the better explanation of regularities. (You might find it helpful to map the probabilities to Figure 4.)

---

[101] Some philosophers, bothered by technical difficulties of assigning probabilities to metaphysical hypotheses, will be wary of such arguments. But sometimes technical problems often have creative solutions. For example, Lazarovici (2020) provides an explanatory argument for Non-Humeanism over Humeanism in terms of "typicality" instead of probability. The fundamental insights are similar, but arguably the notion of typicality is easier to apply to unbounded spaces of possibilities.

[102] You might object: "But what if there are irreducibly probabilistic laws? Won't that mean that any possible Humean mosaic is logically compatible with Non-Humeanism?" Yes. However, irreducibly probabilistic laws would justify a nonuniform probability function over Non-Humean possible worlds. For example, suppose it's a law that each F has a 99 percent chance of being G. Now consider two worlds with exactly 100 Fs. All Fs are Gs in one, whereas no Fs are Gs in the other. The first world deserves a higher prior probability.

7.4 Two Explanatory Problems

I used to think that the argument above was pretty decisive, at least given my background assumptions. However, I now think that the final step – the claim that $P(R|N)$ is reasonably high – contains an important oversight. If you reflect on our discussion of extensional problems for Non-Humeanism in Section 6 you might be able to spot it.

The first problem is directly inspired by the Scientific Criterion. Some Non-Humean theories lack flexibility. For example, property-based theories stipulate that laws have to involve certain kinds of relationships between natural properties. But as we saw in Section 6, the metaphysical structure they invoke can make it difficult to accommodate certain types of laws. If they can't account for such laws, the probability of the relevant regularities given property-based theories turns out to be extremely low.

The second problem runs in the opposite direction. Suppose we tried to explain sequence S in our **Dice** case with one of the following hypotheses:

Trickster Deity, Specific (TDS): There is a powerful demon with a very strong preference for sequence S to occur on this occasion.

Trickster Deity, General (TDG): There's a demon with the power to determine the outcome of rolls of dice.

Neither explanation is a good one. The prior probability $P(TDS)$ is astronomically low, because TDS is such a narrow, specific hypothesis. For exactly the same reason, the likelihood $P(S|TDG)$ is astronomically low. Even if one believes in demons, why think there's a demon with a preference for *that* sequence on this occasion? This new question is just as difficult to answer as the original question "Why sequence S?" In positing this demon, we've simply pushed the explanatory problem back a level.

Divine Voluntarists and Primitivists face an analogous problem. Suppose we ask: Why does God decree regularities as opposed to something else? Why do primitive laws give rise to regularities as opposed to something else? Given how little we've said about God and primitive laws, these questions may seem just as puzzling as the question "Why does our world contain regularities in the first place?"[103] Thus, it is reasonable to wonder whether Divine Voluntarism and Primitivism provide a satisfying explanation of regularities.

---

[103] Here, for example, is an argument that $P(R|PL)$ is just as low as $P(R|H)$. The primitive law operator can attach itself to *any* sentence. But because most possible sentences don't describe regularities, most epistemically possible primitive laws don't give rise to regularities. In addition, because so little has been said about primitive lawhood, there seems to be no reason to think that the operator is more likely to attach to sentences describing regularities than to any other type of sentence. Thus, Primitivism permits a large, diverse set of possible laws, while

It's hard to avoid both explanatory problems. Non-Humean theories with lots of metaphysical structure may not be able to posit sophisticated laws of the sort found in our world. Non-Humean theories with little metaphysical structure may be unable to constrain statements of laws to statements describing regularities. We can't treat Non-Humeanism as a monolithic group of theories whose explanatory power is on par with one another. Different sorts of theories face different explanatory problems. A good explanation of regularities requires the right version of Non-Humeanism. It may be that no such version exists.

7.5 Conclusion

As Section 7.4 suggests, the explanatory argument is difficult to defend. But speaking for myself, I am optimistic that we can walk a line between the two explanatory problems described in this section. I'll briefly mention two paths forward.

First, Tom Metcalf and I defend a solution on behalf of Divine Voluntarists in Hildebrand and Metcalf (2022). The central idea is that God, merely in virtue of being intelligent, is somewhat likely to have preferences for some degree of regularity in nature. For example, states of affairs with moral and aesthetic value – the sorts of things that intelligent beings care about – tend to require underlying regularities in order to be realized in the first place. If that's right, perhaps Divine Voluntarists can offer a principled answer to the question "Why does God decree regularities as opposed to something else?"

Second, consider property-based theories such as DTA or Dispositionalism. Because they posit relations between universals (or natural properties in some sense), they don't have to provide independent motivation for thinking that nomic necessities involve generalizations and thus give rise to some sort of regularities in the long run.[104] But they do have to find a way to make their theories more flexible in order to accommodate the forms of regularities discovered through the actual practice of science in the actual world. In response, suppose that DTA theorists allow any nomic relation that can be specified by a Tooley-style construction function in a language whose fundamental predicates refer to universals. If they didn't place any further restrictions on the contents of construction functions, they would still face a problem of arbitrarily complex construction functions: make a function complex enough and it'll

---

precluding any reason to assign higher probability to some possible laws than others. The structure of the problem is the same as for Humeanism. See Hildebrand (2013) for a more careful defense of this argument.

[104] For my own attempt to argue that property-based theories of laws must give rise to regularities, see Hildebrand (2018).

give rise to irregular worlds even though it has the form of a generalization! However, they might block this implication by proposing a further restriction: nomic relations involving simpler construction functions are just more likely to obtain. (Perhaps this could be motivated by the claim that simplicity of fundamental theoretical posits is a theoretical virtue.) In sum, if statements of law must be written in languages with natural properties, and simpler statements are more likely to obtain than complex ones, then there are good reasons not to worry about arbitrarily complex functions.[105]

These solutions are speculative, of course. However, I think they give us some reason for optimism that Non-Humeanism (or some version anyway) does provide a better explanation of regularities than Humeanism. However, as I mentioned at the outset, this judgment depends on some significant epistemological assumptions as well. In the next section, we'll examine some of them more carefully.

8 Epistemological and Methodological Issues

8.1 Method in Metaphysics

In this section, we'll consider some epistemological and methodological issues that arise for the metaphysics of laws of nature. As you may have noticed, metaphysics is hard. Its questions are general and abstract. Competing metaphysical theories often are, or seem to be, empirically equivalent.

Here is a sample description of a method of practicing metaphysics that is loosely inspired by Quine (1948):

Neo-Quinean Method: Metaphysical theorizing consists of determining which theoretical beliefs best fit within our web of beliefs – a web that is informed, but not wholly determined, by experience. The best fitting theory is the one with the best balance of theoretical virtues such as familiarity of primitives, simplicity, ontological parsimony, explanatory strength, and the like.

This statement is intentionally vague. I want it to be compatible with many specific ways of doing metaphysics. But here are some clarifications.

---

[105] It is worth mentioning that the two constraints suggested here – one concerning natural predicates and one concerning simplicity – align nicely with two constraints proposed by Chen and Goldstein (2022) in their defense of a version of Primitivism. Although Primitivists and property-based theorists start with different perspectives, we may see a convergence of theories as they are updated in response to various explanatory challenges.

First, although I've used the label 'Neo-Quinean', proponents needn't endorse all of Quine's epistemological theses. For example, though my statement above mentions a "web of beliefs," it doesn't require coherentism about the structure of justification. It doesn't require a commitment to empiricism about the sources of justification or Quinean pragmatism either.

Second, I listed some sample criteria for theory choice, but I didn't say which criteria to accept or how to weight them. This should sound familiar. It is essentially the same problem that best systems accounts face in answering the question "What makes a best system *best*?," and it fits the general approach to metaphysics that we are taking in this Element. I've discussed lots of criteria without taking a stand on which ones matter and how they are to be weighted. However, when all is said and done, your choice of theory will be sensitive to your methods.

Third, the method is compatible with different interpretations of criteria for theory choice: They may or may not be *truth-conducive*. Suppose you wish to give your uncle reason to believe that the earth is not flat. On a clear day, you look toward a mountain range that is beyond the horizon when viewed from ground level. As you climb a radio tower together, mountains appear from top to bottom. You have provided your uncle with an *epistemic* reason for belief – a reason to think that the belief in question is *true*. When your uncle grasps this reason, he has *epistemic justification* for believing that the earth isn't flat. Of course, if your dear uncle is afraid of heights, you could try a different approach. Without performing any experiments at all, you could say "If you form the belief that the earth isn't flat I'll give you $1,000." It would be in your uncle's interests to form the belief, but his reason wouldn't have anything to do with the truth value of the claim in question. His reason for belief would be *merely pragmatic*. Similarly, the criteria for theory choice involved in metaphysics can be interpreted in different sorts of ways. Perhaps they aim at the truth, but perhaps they merely serve our interests, promote valuable worldviews, provide comfort, satisfy aesthetic preferences (consider Quine's stated preference for "desert landscapes" (1948, 23)), etc.

Fourth, and most importantly, at least some of our criteria for theory choice are *non-empirical*. I say this because there is a gap between observation and theory. This is the famous *underdetermination problem*: For any empirical observations, there are multiple theories compatible with those observations.[106] Here is a pair of examples to illustrate. First, empirical underdetermination arises in real-world scientific theory choice. The Eddington experiment discussed in Section 1 is an example. Scientists faced a choice between General

---

[106] See Stanford (2021) for an introduction.

Relativity and various modified Newtonian theories that were empirically equivalent with respect to observations of the day. Second, empirical underdetermination drives classic arguments for skepticism. For example, external world skeptics posit empirically equivalent hypotheses about the origin of your experience: The appearance of words on this page might be caused by physical objects in the external world, but they might be caused by an evil demon who wishes to give you exactly the same experiences you'd have if you inhabited a physical world. Obviously, we can't justify one hypothesis over its empirically equivalent competitors purely on the basis of *observation*, since observations are stipulated to be the same across the hypotheses. In situations such as these, we need to appeal to *nonempirical* criteria to choose a theory. They are utterly indispensable.[107]

Another approach to connecting underdetermination to nonempirical criteria for theory choice in the context of metaphysics is simply to examine the methods we've been using in this Element.[108] For example, consider the intensional criteria from Section 3: that laws govern, support counterfactuals, explain their instances, and support induction. Both the criteria and our attempts to apply them to theories seem to involve nonempirical elements. Or consider the explanatory argument for Non-Humeanism discussed in Section 7: The assignment of probabilities, especially of priors, clearly involves nonempirical elements. Or consider the economy criteria that often motivate Humeanism. One such criterion holds that, other things being equal, theories with fewer types of fundamental entities are more likely to be true. It is hard to see how such a criterion could be supported on purely empirical grounds. Moreover, as I hope is clear, reasonable people can disagree about which criteria we ought to use and how they ought to be balanced. Plausibly, the act of *balancing/weighting* such criteria involves nonempirical factors, whichever criteria we prefer.

My point, in short, is that observation (the purely empirical) can't do *all* the heavy lifting in choosing a metaphysical theory. We have to bring something else to the table – something nonempirical – when we engage in theorizing. This is especially the case in metaphysics, given that its problems are so general and abstract.

---

[107] BonJour (1998) provides several arguments for the indispensability of a priori justification. My claim in this section is more modest than his, because I do not claim that nonempirical criteria must be *epistemically* justified.

[108] For arguments that there are indispensable a priori elements for any method of metaphysical theorizing, even those that proceed from our best scientific theories, see Chakravartty (2017) and Tahko (2015, chaps. 7–9).

Although our discussion of methodological issues has been brief, I think it supports two conclusions related to the debate between Humeanism and Non-Humeanism. First, your choice of theory is likely to be highly sensitive to the details of the method you employ. If you place special value on economy, then you may lean towards Humeanism. If you place special value on certain intensional criteria, then you may lean towards Non-Humeanism. Second, the epistemological resources required to support a metaphysical theory are, in an abstract epistemological sense, the same. It does not seem that we can defend a metaphysical thesis like Humeanism by appeal to empiricism about epistemic justification, since Humeans and Non-Humeans alike require nonempirical criteria for theory choice. (I'll say a bit more about this in the next section.) It shouldn't be surprising that the epistemological resources required to support a metaphysical theory of laws are similar in this respect. Both theories make bold, speculative claims about the nature of the world that underlies our experience. After all, they provide competing answers to the very same metaphysical question: "What is the nature of laws?"

We'll now shift gears and consider some questions about our epistemic access to laws. Over the next two subsections we'll examine some epistemological problems for Non-Humeanism and Humeanism, respectively. As the preceding discussion suggests, I'll argue that these problems have a similar character.

8.2 Epistemological Objections to Non-Humeanism

There is an important respect in which Non-Humeanism might seem less modest than Humeanism. Everyone agrees that there are regularities, and that laws have something to do with regularities. Humeans simply identify laws with regularities, whereas Non-Humeans posit some *extra* things required for lawhood. But what is our justification for believing in these extra things? Some philosophers believe that this question cannot be answered. Broadly speaking, there are two different versions of this objection.

8.2.1 A New Worry about Explanatory Arguments

The first version of the objection comes in different varieties, depending on one's preferred method of practicing metaphysics, but I'll focus on one that targets the explanatory argument for Non-Humeanism. As formulated in Section 7, the explanatory argument for Non-Humeanism is supposed to show that its conclusion is *true* – not merely that it would be in our interests to believe it. But as mentioned in Section 7, some of the crucial premises of the explanatory argument rely on nonempirical criteria. Putting these together, the explanatory argument seems to require some nontrivial justification that is independent of experience. In other words, it seems to require *nontrivial a priori justification*. Of course, the rejection of that sort of justification is a central component of Hume's (1748/2000, esp. section 4) brand of *empiricism about epistemic justification*.[109] The worry, in short, is that some of the most influential arguments in favor of Non-Humeanism require a controversial epistemological thesis.

If I had more space, I'd provide an overview of various theories of epistemic justification, and specifically the debate over a priori justification.[110] However, for our purposes, we can sidestep these issues. I have already argued that *everyone* requires nonempirical criteria for theory choice. If Non-Humeans didn't have a special commitment to treating these criteria as truth-conducive, that would suffice to undermine the objection under consideration.

I don't see any reason to believe that Non-Humeans have these special commitments, because we can offer a pragmatist interpretation of the explanatory argument. In Section 7, I suggested that the probabilities featured in the explanatory argument are *objective* epistemic probabilities. We could instead treat them as *subjective* epistemic probabilities. Positing objective constraints on prior probabilities seems to imply that we have some kind of insight into the structure of modal space; positing subjective constraints on priors does not. For example, a subjectivist might adopt the following position:

> I don't claim that everyone should accept the premises of the explanatory argument. Rationality does not require that in general. However, its premises don't violate any constraints on rational assignments of prior probabilities, and as it turns out I happen to accept them. Given my assignment of priors, it's rational for me to have a high credence in Non-Humeanism.

This position seems coherent, and it's compatible with a pragmatist interpretation of metaphysical method generally speaking. Such interpretations aren't for everyone.[111] However, Humeans who interpret their metaphysics pragmatically are not well-positioned to criticize Non-Humeans for doing the same.

There is a broader lesson here. We don't need to settle all the debates of metametaphysics to evaluate first-order theories in metaphysics. Just as both Humeans and Non-Humeans accept nonempirical criteria for theory choice,

---

[109] Hume's denial that there is nontrivial a priori epistemic justification is not at odds with his acceptance of nonempirical criteria for theory choice, given that he interprets the latter pragmatically. I'll say a bit more about this in the final section.

[110] There is a voluminous literature on a priori justification. BonJour (1998), Casullo (2003), and Jenkins (2008) provide good starting points.

[111] See, for example, Bricker (2020).

both have freedom concerning the interpretation of these criteria and of their subsequent metaphysical theories.

8.2.2 A Further Layer of Underdetermination?

Let's turn to a different epistemological objection to Non-Humeanism. Non-Humeanism allows for differences in laws without differences in regularities. This (allegedly) opens the door to a special kind of underdetermination.[112]

Suppose we observe that all Fs are Gs. Here are two ways for the DTA theory to explain this regularity.

(1) There is a fundamental law $N(F, G)$.
(2) F and G are not fundamental. They are derived from some more fundamental universals unknown to us, and the regularity that all Fs are Gs is derived from some nomic relation among these more fundamental universals.

Both (1) and (2) explain the regularity that all Fs are Gs, but they posit different laws and properties. Our choice between them is underdetermined by the observation that all Fs are Gs. The problem, then, is that Non-Humeans cannot claim to have epistemic access to the law itself (whatever it is). But Humeans can, because our epistemic access to regularities is more straightforward. Or so the objection goes.

I see no problem with this sort of underdetermination. It's philosophically interesting, but not because of its connection to the metaphysics of laws. It is simply an example of *scientific underdetermination*. In this situation, the contents of statements of laws differs between the two Non-Humean theories. If F and G are fundamental, the correct statement of law is that *all Fs are Gs*. If F and G are not fundamental, then the correct statement of law will involve the more fundamental properties rather than F and G. As such, the same sort of underdetermination should be allowed by *Humean* theories as well. After all, contemporary Humeans do not take observed regularities to be fundamental. (Observed regularities tend to involve medium-sized objects rather than fundamental points of the mosaic.)

In sum, this type of argument *does* suggest that our epistemic connection to the laws themselves is somewhat weak and tenuous, but I think that's exactly right. We can reasonably worry about the epistemological assumptions required to justify belief in Non-Humean theoretical entities, but, as we'll see in the next subsection, we can reasonably worry about the epistemological assumptions required to justify belief in Humean laws as well.

---

[112] See Earman and Roberts (2005b) for a version of this objection.

8.3 An Epistemological Objection to Humeanism

The underdetermination problem in Section 8.2.2 suggests an epistemological objection to Humeanism. We don't really observe the regularities that Humeans identify with laws. Rather, we observe regularities *in observed parts of nature*. However, statements of laws are not merely statements describing the observed parts of nature. They are statements describing nature as a whole. Thus, even setting aside the gap between regularities among that which we observe and regularities posited to obtain at more fundamental levels of nature, there is a further gap between observed regularities and Humean laws. The same gap holds between the best systematization *of our evidence* and the best systematization *of everything*. Humeans must bridge this gap to justify the claim that we have epistemic access to the laws of nature. But it is a difficult gap to bridge, precisely because it is the same gap that is involved in the problem of induction.

I think it is important to compare this problem with the epistemological challenges we raised against the explanatory argument in Section 8.2. The central problem for the explanatory argument is this: It requires a powerful form of ampliative (nondeductive) inference, which is why it cannot be deployed without adopting nontrivial nonempirical criteria for theory choice. But we have just seen that Humeans face essentially the same problem. They must assume the cogency of a powerful form of ampliative inference as well: that enumerative induction is truth-conducive, that nature is uniform, etc. The question, then, is whether such an assumption can be justified (or motivated on pragmatic grounds). As we discussed in Section 3.4, this is a source of ongoing controversy. For now, I'll simply point out that Humeans do not have an easy answer to this challenge, especially if they don't want to allow Non-Humeans an analogous answer to some of their own epistemological challenges.

8.4 Conclusion

Epistemological questions are important for the metaphysics of laws. Whether we're Humeans or Non-Humeans, we must rely on some nonempirical criteria for theory choice. These can be interpreted in various ways (realistically, pragmatically, etc.). But we have to incorporate them somehow, both to justify a choice of theories in the first place and to explain our justification for believing that there are any laws at all.

To emphasize the difficulty of this task, let's briefly review some of the criteria for a theory of laws that we have discussed thus far. Theories must be internally consistent. Their primitives must be intelligible. They should classify all and only the laws of our best scientific theories (in this world and others) as laws. They should be parsimonious/economical. They should account for intensional criteria: that laws govern, explain, support counterfactuals, support induction, etc. They should fit within our broader metaphysical worldviews. And there are others besides. It is important to recognize that these criteria are not independent of one another with respect to our evaluation of theories of laws. Consider how an axiomatic solution to the inference problem suggests that Non-Humean theories can make sense of governance. Or consider a version of Non-Humeanism that can't make sense of functional laws. According to that theory, the functional "laws" of our best theories aren't really laws: they can't then be said to govern, explain, etc. That would be a serious problem. Or consider the fact that economy criteria contain a *ceteris paribus* clause. To say whether Humeanism is better than Non-Humeanism because its ontology is more economical, we'd first need to show that Non-Humeanism doesn't have advantages with respect to other criteria.

My suspicion, for what it's worth, is that your preference for Humeanism or Non-Humeanism is probably determined in advance by your epistemological preferences. Do you want to justify induction? Are you willing to take explanatory principles for granted? Then you'll probably be inclined towards Non-Humeanism. Do you prefer economical theories? Are you suspicious of modal entities? Then you'll probably be inclined towards Humeanism. We may well have reached an impasse, in which the only path forward is to settle (or at least clarify) the relevant methodological disputes. However, in the final section I'll suggest a different response to this impasse.

9 An Alternative to Humeanism and Non-Humeanism

In Section 8, I argued that justifying any metaphysical theory of laws, Humean or Non-Humean, requires nonempirical criteria for theory choice. When all is said and done, the epistemology of metaphysics is not so different for Humeans and Non-Humeans. This conclusion is somewhat in tension with the Humean goal of striving for epistemological modesty and avoiding metaphysical speculation. As it turns out, there is a more modest, less speculative position available.

9.1 Motivating Humeanism, or Something Else?

Many motivations for Humeanism are inspired by David Hume. We've encountered some already. Notably, we considered Hume's *Concept Empiricism* in Section 5 and his *Empiricism about epistemic justification* in Section 8. However, there is a more general, and perhaps deeper, motivation found in Hume's work. His *Enquiry* doesn't begin with a statement of empiricism. Rather, it begins with a lamentation about metaphysical speculation. We might agree that we are limited in ways that make metaphysics difficult even if we don't agree with Hume's later diagnosis of the human condition and his specific empiricist theses. Thus, even before we diagnose the reasons why we struggle to do metaphysics well, the following position might seem attractive:

(Humean) Minimalism: Metaphysics should be avoided insofar as possible.[113]

After all, metaphysics is abstract, speculative, and difficult. We are seriously limited, so why go to the trouble? Before we proceed, here are some clarifications about this position.

First, do not confuse Minimalism with a criterion of ontological economy. Economy criteria are *metaphysical criteria* that help us to select metaphysical theories. Minimalism tells us to avoid metaphysics.

Second, Minimalism doesn't say that metaphysics *can't* be done, and it doesn't tell us to avoid metaphysics *altogether*. (That wouldn't be very modest.) It might be impossible to avoid metaphysics entirely, especially since certain theoretical and practical projects seem to have at least some ontological commitments.

Third, if we are to embrace Minimalism, we'll need to decide which theoretical projects are essential, as that will determine which parts of metaphysics are unavoidable. This is a general point about Minimalism. I have not yet said anything about how Minimalism relates to laws. However, this gives us an important clue as to how it might.

Suppose we value the sciences. Then we must trust induction, both to establish scientific theories and to apply them to the world. And in particular, we need some way to distinguish between good inductive inferences and bad. To do these things, we have to assume that *nature is uniform*. This claim does not seem to be entirely metaphysically neutral. It's about nature, after all.[114] However, it does *not* require us to take a stand on the debate between Humeanism and Non-Humeanism. The assumption that nature is uniform supports these theoretical and practical projects to some extent regardless of whether (i) we posit Non-Humean whatnots that underlie and explain the principle or (ii) we simply

---

[113] Minimalism admits of different interpretations, but here is a modest one. We could interpret it as a *stance* in van Fraassen's (1980) sense, such that adopting the position amounts to endorsing the following: "I resolve to avoid taking a stand on metaphysical questions unless I have to do so." Thanks to Trevor Teitel for encouraging me to consider different formulations of Minimalism.

[114] Specifically, it might point towards an objective conception of nature. Further, it may require that we give accounts of properties and of the structure of spacetime, since these are involved in our understanding of regularities.

interpret the principle as a brute fact (as Humeans do). Therefore, Minimalists may *not* need to answer questions such as these: Why are there regularities in the first place? Which comes first, the regularities or the laws? They can simply remain neutral. They can be agnostic about the distinction between Humeanism and Non-Humeanism. Although they say something about the world, and so don't avoid metaphysics entirely, they can avoid taking a stand on this metaphysical debate.

9.2 Minimalism about Laws

Our discussion of the principle of uniformity of nature raises an interesting question about Minimalism: Can Minimalists say anything about laws or lawhood?

We began this Element by distinguishing between scientific and metaphysical questions about laws of nature.

Scientific Question: *Which* laws does our world contain?

Metaphysical Question: *What* are laws? Specifically, are they prior to regularities, or vice versa?

Minimalists about laws avoid answering the Metaphysical Question about laws, but that doesn't mean that they have to remain completely silent on the topic of laws. We can ask other philosophical questions about laws. For example:

Methodological Question: What is the best method for answering the Scientific Question about laws?

This isn't the only additional philosophical question we can ask, and I don't claim that it's the most important. But it can help us to answer the question "What can Minimalists say about laws?" They can answer the Methodological Question without committing to an answer to the Metaphysical Question. Here is my official, though somewhat tentative, statement of the view:

Minimalism about Laws: The position of anyone who answers some philosophical questions about laws (such as the Methodological Question) without answering the Metaphysical Question about laws.

This position accommodates Hume's general taste for modesty while allowing that some theoretical and practical projects are unavoidable.[115]

---

[115] Some Hume scholars – notably Strawson (1989) – ascribe the following position to Hume: If there is such a thing as primitive necessity in nature, we aren't in the position to understand it,

For example, suppose one gives an account of which principles of induction we should accept but that their account doesn't appeal to some underlying account of the nature of laws. This might still clarify the concept of laws in some ways. For example, if the principles of induction make reference to laws, they at least serve to clarify the inferential role of laws. Or suppose one articulates some theoretical criteria that guide the selection of scientific theories. In doing so, they seem to provide information about the role that lawhood plays in scientific practice. In both these examples, these answers to the Methodological Question improve our understanding of laws somewhat, even though they answer neither the Scientific Question nor the Metaphysical Question.

This is not to say that the Methodological Question is irrelevant to the Scientific and Metaphysical Questions. Far from it. Better methods lead to better science. And nothing prevents us from inquiring about the metaphysics of laws – for example, by seeking a metaphysical foundation from which we can explain or justify the relevant methodological principles. Those of us who wish to do metaphysics will probably view answers to the Methodological Question as suggesting criteria for a metaphysical theory of laws. However, we can't force everyone to do metaphysics. Minimalists seem within their rights in remaining agnostic about the relevant metaphysical foundations.

9.3 Lessons and Applications

In this subsection, I'll discuss two potential applications of Minimalism about laws and suggest a few general lessons.

To begin, the Methodological Question should sound familiar. It's intimately related to the compulsory question "What makes the best system *best*?" The main difference, I take it, is that theoretical scientists systematize *observed parts* of the mosaic whereas the analysis of laws concerns the systematization of the *entire* mosaic. Consider Pragmatic Humeanism. Its proponents often say that they wish to avoid metaphysics. Their attempts to answer the compulsory question are motivated explicitly by an examination of actual scientific practice in which they operate under the assumption that scientific methods are good methods. And they embrace a degree of subjectivism about lawhood, motivated by the idea that philosophical accounts of laws should explain why laws serve various epistemic and pragmatic ends. Each of these features seems to point to an answer to the Methodological Question about laws.

---

and as a result it is pointless to speculate about it (as Non-Humeans do); however, we should *not* claim that there is no such thing as primitive necessity (as Humeans do) either. By these lights, odd as it may sound, Hume does *not* accept Humeanism about laws of nature. Perhaps we could interpret Hume as a Minimalist about laws instead.

As formulated, these features might also suggest answers to our Meta-physical Question but only when they are augmented by further criteria for metaphysical theory choice. I wonder, then, whether some Pragmatic Humeans would be content simply to answer the Methodological Question while remaining agnostic about the Metaphysical Question. In doing so, they could say something useful about how the concept of law helps to structure scientific practice, while falling short of making further claims about the existence or nonexistence of primitive necessities. This is to say that some "Pragmatic Humeans" might prefer to endorse Minimalism about laws instead of Humeanism. To be clear, I'm not saying that this is how Pragmatic Humeans conceive of their own project.[116] But perhaps they should. Some of the difficult problems this view faces when it is interpreted as a theory about the nature of laws – I'm thinking of both extensional and intensional objections to Humeanism – simply don't apply to Minimalism about laws. At the very least, Minimalism about laws has attractive features that fit nicely with the motivations Pragmatic Humeans claim to provide.[117]

Let's turn to our second application. Here is an obvious fact about statements of laws: They have a certain "modal superstructure," such that they exhibit a high degree of modal stability.[118] Scientists hold laws fixed when building models, evaluating counterfactuals, and making predictions. We might look carefully at scientific practice to identify these modal features: how they relate to mathematical necessities, accidents, meta-laws, etc. It seems to me that articulating these features helps to clarify the concept of law even if it falls short of answering our Metaphysical Question about laws. Thus, merely providing an account of the modal superstructure of laws seems like something a Minimalist about laws might do. To be clear, I'm not claiming that Cartwright, Lange, and Woodward endorse Minimalism about laws. I am just claiming that it fits well with some of their stated motivations. To be sure, one can use these facts about modal superstructure – conceived here as answers to the Methodological Question about laws – as providing *criteria* for metaphysical theories of laws. (Lange does this explicitly.) But one might rest content merely to answer the Methodological Question in terms of modal superstructure and stop there.

---

[116] Though recently some, for example Loewer (2021), have attempted to minimize the Humean elements of their position.

[117] I'm not the first to suggest that Humeans might wish to reconceptualize their own position in a less metaphysically loaded way. See Ismael (2015) and Fernandes (in press) for other proposals to this effect. I'm not sure whether they would recommend that Humeans adopt Minimalism as I've defined it, but their proposals have a similar character.

[118] This is a major theme in the work of Cartwright (1999), Lange (2009), and Woodward (2018).

Here is a general lesson. In both examples of Minimalism about laws, we mentioned the possibility that answers to the Methodological Question might be relevant to the metaphysics of laws. However, there's a gap between the Methodological and Metaphysical Questions. There are many ways to bridge this gap, depending on the details of one's preferred methodology for metaphysics. All practice-based arguments require some sort of bridge – a link that takes us from Method to Metaphysics. For example, suppose we notice that scientists are happy to assume that nature is uniform. A principle of ontological parsimony might motivate Humeanism, whereas certain explanatory principles might motivate Non-Humeanism. As we discussed in Section 8, any such bridge will be controversial. Establishing any such link would violate the spirit of Minimalism.

Generally speaking, I think we should exercise caution when evaluating metaphysical arguments based on scientific practice. Pragmatic Humeans have done excellent work in articulating criteria for theory choice that feature in scientific practice. However, I am not convinced by their arguments that these criteria really motivate Humeanism, because I think Non-Humeans can tell good stories about how the relevant scientific methods and criteria for theory choice are supported and explained by their own position on the metaphysics of laws. For similar reasons, I doubt that accounts of the modal superstructure of laws push us in the direction of Non-Humeanism. On the surface, they seem to fit nicely with Non-Humeanism, since they involve modally rich concepts. However, Humeans can tell good stories about how these modal claims fit within their general picture of natural modality as well.

9.4 Conclusion

I can't require anyone to ask metaphysical questions about laws. Some people might prefer to ask other questions. That's fine. It's possible to focus on the Scientific Question without worrying about the Metaphysical Question. Scientists do this all the time. It's possible to focus on the Methodological Question without worrying about the Metaphysical Question. Philosophers of science and epistemologists do this all the time. However, this doesn't mean that Metaphysical Questions aren't good questions, aren't important questions, or aren't questions we are capable of answering. Once we start asking philosophical questions, including the Methodological Question about laws, it's hard to draw a line and argue that we cannot or should not ask Metaphysical Questions.

In parting, let me offer a final assessment of the overall debate concerning the metaphysics of laws. If there is a crucial issue, it is this: *Can Non-Humeans deliver on their promises to provide theories that do what we want theories of laws to do – to satisfy the criteria we take to be important better than Humean theories?* If so, considerations of ontological economy won't come into play, and Humeanism will be very difficult to motivate. (Some historical motivations for Humeanism are now out of vogue; others are ill-fated; and others motivate Minimalism rather than Humeanism.) If not, we could embrace either Humeanism if we value economy criteria or Minimalism about laws if we prefer to avoid metaphysics. Of course, to evaluate this crucial question, we need to examine the theories and review the arguments. In other words, we have to actually do the metaphysics. I hope that this Element has provided a foundation for you to do just that.

References

Adams, D. (2018). God and dispositional essentialism: An account of the laws of nature. *Pacific Philosophical Quarterly*, *99*(2), 293–316.

Adlam, E. (2022). Laws of nature as constraints. *Foundations of Physics*, *52*(28), 1–41.

Anjum, R. L., & Mumford, S. (2018). *What tends to be: The philosophy of dispositional modality*. London and New York: Routledge.

Anscombe, G. (1971). *Causality and determination*. Cambridge: Cambridge University Press.

Aquinas. (1972). *De veritate. An Aquinas reader* (M. Clark, Ed.). New York: Fordham University Press.

Armstrong, D. (1983). *What is a law of nature?* Cambridge: Cambridge University Press.

Armstrong, D. (1989a). *A combinatorial theory of possibility*. Cambridge: Cambridge University Press.

Armstrong, D. (1989b). *Universals: An opinionated introduction*. Boulder, CO: Westview Press.

Armstrong, D. (1997). *A world of states of affairs*. Cambridge: Cambridge University Press.

Barker, S., & Smart, B. (2012). The ultimate argument against dispositional monist accounts of laws. *Analysis*, *72*(4), 714–722.

Bechtel, W., & Abrahamsen, A. (2005). Explanation: A mechanistic alternative. *Studies in History and Philosophy of Biological and Biological Sciences*, *36*, 421–441.

Beebee, H. (2000). The non-governing conception of laws of nature. *Philosophy and Phenomenological Research*, *61*(3), 571–594.

Beebee, H. (2011). Necessary connections and the problem of induction. *Noûs*, *45*(3), 504–527.

Bhogal, H. (2020a). Humeanism about laws of nature. *Philosophy Compass*, *15*(8), 1–10.

Bhogal, H. (2020b). Nomothetic explanation and Humeanism about laws of nature. In K. Bennett & D. Zimmerman (Eds.), *Oxford studies in metaphysics* (Vol. 12, pp. 164–202). Oxford: Oxford University Press.

Bhogal, H., & Perry, Z. (2017). What the Humean should say about entanglement. *Noûs*, *51*(1), 74–94.

Bigelow, J., Ellis, B., & Lierse, C. (1992). The world as one of a kind: Natural necessity and laws of nature. *British Journal for the Philosophy of Science, 43*(3), 371–388.

Bird, A. (2005). The ultimate argument against Armstrong's contingent necessitation view of laws. *Analysis, 65,* 147–155.

Bird, A. (2007). *Nature's metaphysics: Laws and properties.* Oxford: Oxford University Press.

Bird, A. (2018). The metaphysics of natural kinds. *Synthese, 195,* 1397–1426.

Bird, A., & Hawley, K. (2011). What are natural kinds? *Philosophical Perspectives, 25*(1), 205–221.

BonJour, L. (1998). *In defense of pure reason.* Cambridge: Cambridge University Press.

Braddon-Mitchell, D. (2001). Lossy laws. *Noûs, 35*(2), 260–277.

Bricker, P. (2020). Realism without parochialism. In *Modal matters: Essays in metaphysics* (pp. 40–76). Oxford: Oxford University Press.

Briggs, R. (2009). The anatomy of the big bad bug. *Noûs, 43*(3), 428–449.

Carroll, J. (1994). *Laws of nature.* Cambridge: Cambridge University Press.

Cartwright, N. (1999). *The dappled world: Boundaries of science.* Cambridge: Cambridge University Press.

Casullo, A. (2003). *A priori justification.* Oxford: Oxford University Press.

Chakravartty, A. (2007). *A metaphysics for scientific realism.* Cambridge: Cambridge University Press.

Chakravartty, A. (2017). *Scientific ontology: Integrating naturalized metaphysics and voluntarist epistemology.* New York: Oxford University Press.

Chen, E. K. (in press). The past hypothesis and the nature of physical laws. In B. Loewer, E. Winsberg, & B. Weslake (Eds.), *Time's arrows and the probability structure of the world.* Cambridge, MA: Harvard University Press.

Chen, E. K., & Goldstein, S. (2022). Governing without a fundamental direction of time: Minimal primitivism about laws of nature. In Y. Ben-Menahem (Ed.), *Rethinking laws of nature* (pp. 21–64). Cham: Springer.

Coates, A. (2020). Making sense of powerful qualities. *Synthese, 198*(9), 8347–8363.

Coates, A. (2021). Essence and the inference problem. *Synthese, 198,* 915–931.

Coates, A. (2022). Tropes, unmanifested dispositions, and powerful qualities. *Erkenntnis, 87,* 2143–2160.

Coates, A. (in press). The primitivist response to the inference problem. *Dialectica.*

Cohen, J., & Callender, C. (2009). A better best system account of lawhood. *Philosophical Studies, 145*, 1–34.

Collins, R. (2009). God and the laws of nature. *Philo, 12*(2), 142–171.

Cowling, S. (2017). *Abstract entities*. New York: Routledge.

Dasgupta, S. (2016). Metaphysical rationalism. *Noûs, 50*(2), 379–418.

Dasgupta, S. (2018). Realism and the absence of value. *Philosophical Review, 127*(3), 279–322.

Demarest, H. (2016). Fundamental properties and the laws of nature. *Philosophy Compass, 10*(5), 334–344.

Demarest, H. (2017). Powerful properties, powerless laws. In J. Jacobs (Ed.), *Causal powers* (pp. 38–53). Oxford: Oxford University Press.

Descartes, R. (1984). *The philosophical writings of Descartes* (Vol. 3; J. Cottingham, R. Stoothoff, D. Murdoch, & A. Kenny, Eds.). New York: Cambridge University Press.

Dolbeault, J. (2017). Laws of nature of panpsychism. *Journal of Consciousness Studies, 24*, 87–110.

Dorst, C. (2018). Toward a best predictive system account of laws of nature. *British Journal for the Philosophy of Science.* https://doi.org/10.1093/hjps/axy016.

Dorst, C. (2022). Why do the laws support counterfactuals? *Erkenntnis, 87*(2), 545–566.

Dosanjh, R. (2021). Laws of nature and individuals. *Philosophy, 96*(1), 49–72.

Draper, P. (2017). God, evil, and the nature of light. In C. Meister & P. K. Moser (Eds.), *The Cambridge companion to the problem of evil* (pp. 69–84). Cambridge: Cambridge University Press.

Dretske, F. (1977). Laws of nature. *Philosophy of Science, 44*(2), 248–268.

Drewery, A. (2005). Essentialism and the necessity of the laws of nature. *Synthese, 144*, 381–396.

Dumsday, T. (2013). Laws of nature don't *have* ceteris paribus clauses, they *are* ceteris paribus clauses. *Ratio, 26*(2), 134–147.

Dumsday, T. (2019). *Dispositionalism and the metaphysics of science*. Cambridge: Cambridge University Press.

Earman, J., & Roberts, J. (1999). *Ceteris paribus*, there is no problem of provisos. *Synthese, 118*, 439–478.

Earman, J., & Roberts, J. T. (2005a). Contact with the nomic: A challenge for deniers of Humean supervenience about laws of nature. Part I: Humean supervenience. *Philosophy and Phenomenological Research, 71*(1), 1–22.

Earman, J., & Roberts, J. T. (2005b). Contact with the nomic: A challenge for deniers of Humean supervenience about laws of nature. Part II: The epistemological argument for Humean supervenience. *Philosophy and Phenomenological Research, 71*(2), 253–286.

Eddon, M., & Meacham, C. (2015). No work for a theory of universals. In B. Loewer & J. Schaffer (Eds.), *A companion to David Lewis* (pp. 116–137). Malden, MA: Wiley-Blackwell.

Ellis, B. (2001). *Scientific essentialism*. Cambridge: Cambridge University Press.

Emery, N. (2017). A naturalist's guide to objective chance. *Philosophy of Science, 84*, 480–499.

Emery, N. (2019). Laws and their instances. *Philosophical Studies, 176*(6), 1535–1561.

Fales, E. (1990). *Causation and universals*. New York: Routledge.

Fernandes, A. (in press). Naturalism, functionalism and chance: Not a best fit for the Humean. In M. Hicks, S. Jaag, & C. Loew (Eds.), *Humean laws for human agents*. Oxford: Oxford University Press.

Filomeno, A. (2019). Are non-accidental regularities a cosmic coincidence? Revisiting a central threat to Humean laws. *Synthese*. https://doi.org/ 10.1007/s11229-019-02397-1.

Foster, J. (2004). *The divine lawmaker*. Oxford: Oxford University Press.

French, S. (2014). *The structure of the world: Metaphysics and representation*. Oxford: Oxford University Press.

Friend, T. (2022). The Humean pragmatic turn and the case for revisionary best systems accounts. *European Journal for Philosophy of Science, 72*(11), 1–26.

Friend, T. (in press). How to be a Humean about symmetries. *British Journal for the Philosophy of Science*.

Goodman, N. (1955). *Fact, fiction, and forecast*. Cambridge, MA: Harvard University Press.

Hàjek, A. (2019). Interpretations of probability. In E. N. Zalta (Ed.), *The Stanford encyclopedia of philosophy* (Fall 2019 ed.). https://plato.stanford .edu/archives/fall2019/entries/probability-interpret/.

Hall, N. (2004). Two mistakes about credence and chance. *Australasian Journal of Philosophy, 82*, 93–111.

Hall, N. (2015). Humean reductionism about laws of nature. In B. Loewer & J. Schaffer (Eds.), *A companion to David Lewis* (pp. 262–277). Malden, MA: Wiley-Blackwell.

Hattab, H. (2018). Early modern roots of the philosophical concept of a law of nature. In W. Ott & L. Patton (Eds.), *Laws of nature* (pp. 18–41). New York: Oxford University Press.

Heil, J. (2003). *From an ontological point of view*. Oxford: Oxford University Press.

Hicks, M. T. (2018). Dynamic Humeanism. *British Journal for the Philosophy of Science, 69*(4), 983–1007.

Hicks, M. T. (2019). What everyone should say about symmetries. *Philosophy of Science, 86*(5), 1284–1294.

Hicks, M. T. (2021). Breaking the explanatory circle. *Philosophical Studies, 178*(2), 533–557.

Hicks, M. T., & Schaffer, J. (2017). Derivative properties in fundamental laws. *British Journal for the Philosophy of Science, 68*, 411–450.

Hicks, M. T., & van Elswyk, P. (2015). Humean laws and circular explanation. *Philosophical Studies, 172*(2), 433–443.

Hildebrand, T. (2013). Can primitive laws explain? *Philosophers' Imprint, 13*(15), 1–15.

Hildebrand, T. (2016). Two types of quidditism. *Australasian Journal of Philosophy, 94*(3), 516–532.

Hildebrand, T. (2018). Natural properties, necessary connections, and the problem of induction. *Philosophy and Phenomenological Research, 96*(3), 668–689.

Hildebrand, T. (2019a). Naturalness constraints on best systems accounts of laws. *Ratio, 32*(3), 163–172.

Hildebrand, T. (2019b). Scientific practice and the epistemology of governing laws. *Journal of the American Philosophical Association, 5*(2), 174–188.

Hildebrand, T. (2020a). Individuation and explanation: A problem for dispositionalism. *Philosophical Studies, 177*, 3863–3883.

Hildebrand, T. (2020b). Non-Humean theories of natural necessity. *Philosophy Compass, 15*(5), 1–14.

Hildebrand, T. (2020c). Platonic laws of nature. *Canadian Journal of Philosophy, 50*(3), 365–381.

Hildebrand, T., & Metcalf, T. (2022). The nomological argument for the existence of God. *Noûs, 56*, 443–472. https://doi.org/10.1111/nous.12364.

Hoffman, J., & Rosenkrantz, G. (2022). Omnipotence. In E. N. Zalta (Ed.), *The Stanford encyclopedia of philosophy* (Spring 2022 ed.). https://plato.stanford.edu/archives/spr2022/entries/omnipotence/.

Huemer, M. (2017). There is no pure empirical reasoning. *Philosophy and Phenomenological Research, 93*(3), 592–613.

Hume, D. (1748/2000). *An enquiry concerning human understanding: Critical edition* (Tom L. Beauchamp, Ed.). Oxford: Clarendon Press.

Ioannidis, S., Livianos, V., & Psillos, S. (2021). No laws and (thin) powers in, no (governing) laws out. *European Journal for Philosophy of Science*, *11*(6), 1–26.

Ismael, J. (2015). How to be Humean. In B. Loewer & J. Schaffer (Eds.), A *companion to David Lewis* (pp. 188-205). Malden, MA: Wiley-Blackwell.

Jaag, S., & Loew, C. (2018). Making best systems *Best for Us. Synthese.* https://doi.org/10.1007/s11229-018-1829-1.

Jacobs, J. (2011). Powerful qualities, not pure powers. *The Monist*, *94*(1), 81–102.

Jenkins, C. (2008). A priori knowledge: Debates and developments. *Philosophy Compass*, *3*(3), 436–450.

Keinanen, M., & Tahko, T. (2019). Bundle theory with kinds. *The Philosophical Quarterly*, *69*(277), 838–857.

Kimpton-Nye, S. (2017). Humean laws in an unHumean world. *Journal of the American Philosophical Association*, *3*(2), 129–147.

Kimpton-Nye, S. (2021). Reconsidering the dispositional essentialist canon. *Philosophical Studies*, *178*, 3421–3441.

Kistler, M. (2006). *Causation and laws of nature*. London and New York: Routledge.

Kment, B. (2014). *Modality and explanatory reasoning*. Oxford: Oxford University Press.

Koslicki, K. (2013). Ontological dependence: An opinionated survey. In B. Schneiter, M. Hoeltje, & A. Steinberg (Eds.), *Varieties of dependence: Ontological dependence, grounding, supervenience, response-dependence (basic philosophical concepts)* (pp. 31–64). Munich: Philosophia Verlag.

Kovacs, D. M. (2020). The oldest solution to the circularity problem for Humeanism about laws of nature. *Synthese*, *198*(9), 1–21.

Lange, M. (1995). Are there natural laws concerning particular biological species? *The Journal of Philosophy*, *92*(8), 430–451.

Lange, M. (2009). *Laws and lawmakers*. Oxford: Oxford University Press.

Lange, M. (2013). Grounding, scientific explanation, and Humean laws. *Philosophical Studies*, *164*, 255–261.

Lange, M. (2018). Transitivity, self-explanation, and the explanatory circularity argument against Humean accounts of natural law. *Synthese*, *195*(3), 1337–1353.

Laplace, P.-S. (1814/1999). *A philosophical essay on probabilities* (Andrew Dale, Ed. and Trans.). New York: Springer.

Lazarovici, D. (2020). Typical Humean worlds have no laws [preprint]. http://philsci-archive.pitt.edu/17469/.

Lewis, D. (1973). *Counterfactuals*. Cambridge, MA: Harvard University Press.

Lewis, D. (1983). New work for a theory of universals. *Australasian Journal of Philosophy, 61*(4), 343–377.

Lewis, D. (1986a). *On the plurality of worlds*. Oxford: Blackwell.

Lewis, D. (1986b). *Philosophical papers* (Vol. 2). Oxford: Oxford University Press.

Lewis, D. (1994). Humean supervenience debugged. *Mind, 412,* 473–490.

Lewis, D. (1999). *Papers in metaphysics and epistemology*. Cambridge: Cambridge University Press.

Locke, J. (1689/1975). *The Clarendon edition of the works of John Locke: An essay concerning human understanding* (P. H. Nidditch, Ed.). Oxford: Oxford University Press.

Loewer, B. (1996). Humean supervenience. *Philosophical Topics, 24,* 101–127.

Loewer, B. (2007). Laws and natural properties. *Philosophical Topics, 35*(1–2), 313–328.

Loewer, B. (2021). The package deal account of laws and properties (PDA). *Synthese, 199,* 1065–1089.

Lowe, E. (1989). *Kinds of being*. New York: Basil Blackwell.

Lowe, E. (2006). *The four-category ontology*. New York: Oxford University Press.

Manson, N. A. (2009). The fine-tuning argument. *Philosophy Compass, 4*(1), 271–286.

Maudlin, T. (2007). *The metaphysics within physics*. Oxford: Oxford University Press.

McKenzie, K. (2022). *Fundamentality and grounding*. Cambridge: Cambridge University Press.

Mellor, D. (2005). *Probability: A philosophical introduction*. New York: Routledge.

Mill, J. S. (1875/1987). *A system of logic*. London: Longmans.

Miller, E. (2015). Humean scientific explanation. *Philosophical Studies, 172*(5), 1311–1332.

Mitchell, S. D. (2000). Dimensions of scientific law. *Philosophy of Science, 67*(2), 242–265.

Molnar, G. (1969). Kneale's argument revisited. *The Philosophical Review, 78*(1), 79–89.

Molnar, G. (2003). *Powers: A study in metaphysics* (S. Mumford, Ed.). Oxford: Oxford University Press.

Mumford, S. (2004). *Laws in nature*. London: Routledge.

Newton, I. (2014). *Philosophical writings: Revised edition* (A. Janiak, Ed.). Cambridge: Cambridge University Press.

Oderberg, D. S. (2007). *Real essentialism.* New York: Routledge.

Ott, W. (2009). *Causation and laws of nature in early modern philosophy.* Oxford: Oxford University Press.

Ott, W., & Patton, L. (2018). Intuitions and assumptions in the debate over laws of nature. In W. Ott & L. Patton (Eds.), *Laws of nature* (pp. 1–17). New York: Oxford University Press.

Paul, L. A. (2012). Metaphysics as modeling: The handmaiden's tale. *Philosophical Studies, 160*(1), 1–29.

Psillos, S. (2018). Laws and powers in the *Frame of Nature.* In W. Ott & L. Patton (Eds.), *Laws of nature* (pp. 80–107). New York: Oxford University Press.

Quine, W. (1948). On what there is. *Review of Metaphysics, 2,* 21–38.

Quine, W. (1951). Two dogmas of empiricism. *The Philosophical Review, 60,* 20–43.

Ramsey, F. (1978). Universals of law and of fact. In D. Mellor (Ed.), *Foundations,* (pp. 128–132). London and Henley: Routledge and Kegan Paul.

Raven, M. (2015). Ground. *Philosophy Compass, 10*(5), 322–333.

Reutlinger, A., Schurz, G., Hüttemann, A., & Jaag, S. (2021). *Ceteris Paribus* laws. In E. N. Zalta (Ed.), *The Stanford encyclopedia of philosophy* (Fall 2021 ed.). https://plato.stanford.edu/archives/fall2021/entries/ceteris-paribus/.

Roberts, J. (2008). *The law-governed universe.* Oxford: Oxford University Press.

Rodriguez-Pereyra, G. (2002). *Resemblance nominalism.* Oxford: Clarendon Press.

Ruby, J. E. (1986). The origins of scientific "law." *Journal of the History of Ideas, 47*(3), 341–359.

Sánchez, V. G. (in press). From nomic Humeanism to normative relativism. *Philosophical Perspectives.*

Schaffer, J. (2016). It is the business of laws to govern. *Dialectica, 70*(4), 577–588.

Schrenk, M. (2006). A theory for special science laws. In H. Bohse & S. Walter (Eds.), *Selected papers contributed to the sections of gap 6, sixth international conference for the society of analytical philosophy.* Paderborn: Mentis.

Schrenk, M. (2010). The powerlessness of necessity. *Noûs, 44*(4), 725–739.

Schrenk, M. (2017). The emergence of better best system laws. *Journal for the General Philosophy of Science, 48,* 469–483.

Schurz, G. (2011). Review of *Nature's Metaphysics: Laws and Properties. Erkenntnis, 74,* 137–142.

Segal, A. (2020). Humeanisms: Metaphysical and epistemological. *Synthese,* *199*(1–2), 905–925.

Sellars, W. (1956). Empiricism and the philosophy of mind. In H. Feigl & M. Scriven (Eds.), *Minnesota studies in the philosophy of science* (Vol. 1, pp. 253–329). Minneapolis: University of Minnesota Press.

Shoemaker, S. (1980). Causality and properties. In P. van Inwagen (Ed.), *Time and cause.* Dordrecht: D. Reidel Publishing.

Shumener, E. (2019). Laws of nature, explanation, and semantic circularity. *British Journal for the Philosophy of Science, 70*(3), 787–815.

Shumener, E. (in press). The power to govern. *Philosophical Perspectives.*

Sider, T. (2011). *Writing the book of the world.* Oxford: Oxford University Press.

Skow, B. (2016). *Reasons why.* Oxford: Oxford University Press.

Stanford, K. (2021). Underdetermination of scientific theory. In E. N. Zalta (Ed.), *The Stanford encyclopedia of philosophy* (Winter 2021 ed.). https://plato.stanford.edu/archives/win2021/entries/scientific-underdete rmination/.

Strawson, G. (1989). *The secret connexion: Causation, realism, and David Hume.* Oxford: Oxford University Press.

Strawson, G. (2015). Humeanism. *Journal of the American Philosophical Association, 1*(1), 96–102.

Swinburne, R. (2006). Relations between universals, or divine laws? *Australasian Journal of Philosophy, 84*(2), 179–189.

Swoyer, C. (1982). The nature of natural laws. *Australasian Journal of Philosophy, 60*(3), 203–223.

Tahko, T. (2015). *An introduction to metametaphysics.* Cambridge: Cambridge University Press.

Tahko, T. (2021). *Unity of science.* Cambridge: Cambridge University Press.

Tan, P. (2020). Ideal laws, counterfactual preservation, and the analyses of lawhood. *Australasian Journal of Philosophy, 98*(3), 574–589.

Tooley, M. (1977). The nature of laws. *Canadian Journal of Philosophy, 7*(4), 667–698.

Tooley, M. (2011). The skeptical challenges of Hume and Berkeley: Can they be answered? *Proceedings of the American Philosophical Association, 85*(2), 27–46.

Tugby, M. (2013a). Graph-theoretic models of dispositional structures. *International Studies in the Philosophy of Science, 27*(1), 23–39.

Tugby, M. (2013b). Platonic dispositionalism. *Mind, 122*(486), 451–480.

Tugby, M. (2017). The problem of retention. *Synthese, 194*(6), 2053–2075.

Tugby, M. (2021). Grounding theories of powers. *Synthese, 198*(12), 11187–11216.

van Cleve, J. (2018). Brute necessity. *Philosophy Compass, 13*, 1–43.

van Fraassen, B. (1980). *The scientific image*. Oxford: Oxford University Press.

van Fraassen, B. (1989). *Laws and symmetry*. Oxford: Clarendon Press.

Vetter, B. (2009). Review of *Nature's Metaphysics: Laws and Properties*. *Logical Analysis and History of Philosophy, 12*, 320–328.

Vetter, B. (2012). Dispositional essentialism and the laws of nature. In A. Bird, B. Ellis, & H. Sankey (Eds.), *Properties, powers, and structures: Issues in the metaphysics of realism*. New York: Routledge.

Vogt, L. (2022). Nominalist dispositional essentialism. *Synthese, 200*(156), 1–29.

Wang, J. (2016). The nature of properties: Causal essentialism. *Philosophy Compass, 11*(3), 168–176.

Weisberg, J. (2019). *Odds and ends: Introducing probability and decision theory with a visual emphasis*. https://jonathanweisberg.org/vip/.

Whittle, A. (2009). Causal nominalism. In T. Handfield (Ed.), *Dispositions and causes* (pp. 242–285). Oxford: Clarendon Press.

Williams, N. (2019). *The powers metaphysic*. New York: Oxford University Press.

Wilsch, T. (2021). Governing laws of nature: Guidance and production. *Philosophical Studies, 178*(3), 909–933.

Wilson, J. (2010). What is Hume's dictum, and why believe it? *Philosophy and Phenomenological Research, 80*, 595–637.

Wilson, M. (1987). What is a law of nature? (book review). *The Philosophical Review, 96*(3), 435–441.

Woodward, J. (2018). Laws: An invariance-based account. In W. Ott & L. Patton (Eds.), *Laws of nature* (pp. 158–180). New York: Oxford University Press.

Acknowledgments

I am deeply indebted to many people. Erica Shumener, Tom Metcalf, Eddy Chen, Harjit Bhogal, Mike Hicks, and two anonymous referees provided detailed and incisive comments on the complete manuscript. My seminar students in the fall of 2021 read an early draft and provided invaluable advice about what worked and what didn't. Tuomas E. Tahko, the series editor, provided help and guidance throughout the process. Audiences at the 2022 Central Division Meeting of the American Philosophical Association, Dalhousie University, and the University of Toronto offered excellent feedback on some of the more original components of the manuscript. In general, my thinking about laws has been influenced by too many people to mention, but my dissertation advisor, Michael Tooley, deserves special recognition. Finally, I couldn't have written this without love, encouragement, and support from Sara, Charlie, and Grant.

Cambridge Elements ☰

Metaphysics

Tuomas E. Tahko
University of Bristol

Tuomas E. Tahko is Professor of Metaphysics of Science at the University of Bristol, UK. Tahko specializes in contemporary analytic metaphysics, with an emphasis on methodological and epistemic issues: 'meta-metaphysics'. He also works at the interface of metaphysics and philosophy of science: 'metaphysics of science'. Tahko is the author of *Unity of Science* (Cambridge University Press, 2021, *Elements in Philosophy of Science*), *An Introduction to Metametaphysics* (Cambridge University Press, 2015) and editor of *Contemporary Aristotelian Metaphysics* (Cambridge University Press, 2012).

About the Series

This highly accessible series of Elements provides brief but comprehensive introductions to the most central topics in metaphysics. Many of the Elements also go into considerable depth, so the series will appeal to both students and academics. Some Elements bridge the gaps between metaphysics, philosophy of science, and epistemology.

Cambridge Elements ≡

Metaphysics